Sell Up & Sail Away

Sell Up & Sail Away

by

MJ Kobernus

NORDLAND
www.nordlandpublishing.com

Copyright

The motif that appears in the chapter headings in this book is a 'galdrastafur' or Icelandic stave known as Vegvísir. It comes from the Huld Manuscript where it was described in the following manner:

"Beri maður stafi þessa á sér villist maður ekki í hríðum né vondu veðri þó ókunnugur sá."

This can be translated as "If a man carries this sign with him, he won't get lost in storms or bad weather, even though in unfamiliar surroundings."

My thanks to Monica Hansebakken for the charcoal rendering of the stave that I have used throughout.

ISBN Print: 978-82-8331-031-3
ISBN E-book: 978-82-8331-028-3

Disclaimer

This book contains the author's own experiences while living in the United States of America, Great Britain and Norway. They reflect his opinions relating to those experiences. Some names and identifying details of individuals mentioned in this book have been changed to protect their privacy, except of course where he specifically wants to embarrass someone.

Dedication

For all those who dream of the sea.

Full fathom five thy father lies;
Of his bones are coral made;
Those are pearls that were his eyes:
Nothing of him that doth fade
But doth suffer a sea-change
Into something rich and strange.
Sea-nymphs hourly ring his knell
Hark! Now I hear them – Ding-dong, bell.

The Tempest, Act I, Sc. II

CONTENTS

Introduction

Hello, and welcome to *Sell up & Sail Away*. This is my personal story about getting it wrong and maybe one day getting it right. But before we start, let's clear up any potential misconceptions. I am not an expert on sailing or cruising, a fact that will become abundantly clear as you read on. In fact, you could say that I am something of a failure. Twice I have tried to set sail into the sunset, and twice I got no further than the dock. So, don't expect a lot of tips on how to deploy a drogue in high seas, or where to get the best deal on fuel in the Bahamas because you won't find it here.

But before you put this book down and choose one that promises shipwrecks and storms, have a little faith. Unless you are very lucky, you will probably face many of the same roadblocks that afflicted me, whether they be related to work, finances or family.

To help you out, this book contains strategies on coping with some of those challenges. I used these strategies to good effect and I hope you will too.

Twice I committed myself to living a different way of life, choosing minimalism over materialism, freedom over financial security. However, both times I was sucked back into the world of money, houses, cars and careers. The reason for my retrograde step both times was ultimately the same; conflicting desires with my partners.

I do not lay any blame on them, after all, the decision to give up the life I wanted was also mine. However, it is necessary to acknowledge the obligation that having a family imposes. Taking care of one's family overrides everything else, including one's own desires or happiness.

This has been a significant motivation for me and it has influenced every decision I have made since I was married, and even more so since I became a father.

If you have kids, you probably know what I am talking about. I bring this up not to elicit sympathy, but rather to highlight the conflict that may exist in your heart just as it did in mine. After all, the desire to provide for one's family and the desire to follow one's dream are rarely simpatico objectives.

A reluctant spouse or significant other who does not understand 'the dream' may be the biggest problem that you will face in your journey. After all, how do you convince your other half that selling everything you own and living in a barrel is a good idea?

But if you are supremely blessed and your partner shares your vision, there will still be other issues that stop you from leaving it all behind. These are the practicalities of life. What to do with your stuff? What to do about work and money? And how will you handle the stresses of living in a tiny space?

Do not despair. Yes, there are definitely a good many hurdles standing between you and the sea, but they are not insurmountable. For every problem, there *is* a solution.

And that is what this book is all about; making your dream a reality in spite of the daily challenges and *in spite of yourself*. After all, if truth be told, the only thing standing between you and your dream, *is* you.

There is no definitive path, no 'one size fits all' approach. I wish I could give you a formula for success or that I could define the necessary character traits that separate the armchair sailor from those who go out and do it.

I cannot. I do not claim to have the answer. All I can do is tell you what I did, and how I approached things. To a very large degree my methods worked for me. Maybe they will work for you too?

But first, a little background on myself. Originally, I am from the United States (Chicago, to be specific) but I grew up in the United Kingdom of Great Britain. At the time of writing this book, I am living and working in Norway, where I have been for almost twenty years. And although I have traveled widely, my wanderlust is not sated and I still feel the call to see more of our wonderful planet.

I make it sound as if I have been jet setting around the world, but that is far from the case. I grew up in poverty in the UK, the third child of four to a single parent. Along with my siblings, I went to the local state school, where I excelled at doing nothing.

Like many kids in the seventies I wore 'hand me downs.' I learned to make do and improvise with what I had. When I left school at sixteen, I saw my life as a series of dead-end, minimum wage jobs. I did not anticipate the future that awaited, but I knew that I was not going to be content to be a wage slave. However, I had no qualifications, was not good at anything and I had zero prospects.

While my friends were sniffing glue and getting involved in petty (and not so petty) crime, I turned to books to provide an escape.

Books can be dangerous. They fill our heads with ideas. They challenge our preconceptions and occasionally they give us the incentive to *actually do*

4

something.

It may be that the books I read as a teenager gave me the incentive to do more, be more and ultimately *want* more from life.

There is a long running philosophical debate about nature versus nurture. In simplistic terms (so that I can understand them) it goes something like this: Are we who we are because of our learned experiences, or have we inherited our personality? In other words, are we the sum of our genes or our experiences?

It is a little like the chicken and egg dilemma, as I do not know which came first. When I try to understand just what is it that drives me to want a life that is, let's be frank, perilous and hard, I wonder if my rootless nature is the result of my early life experiences.

Maybe it is nature *and* nurture. Or, as my mother would say, it's 'six of one, and half a dozen of the other.'

Working on the premise that my life experiences are part of the underlying reason that I want to be a cruising sailor, I have included personal anecdotes from my past that I believe have helped shape my world view. If you do not think these interludes are interesting, by all means just skip them. Of course, you will miss some exciting and amusing stories, but that is just my opinion.

Now, go put on a raincoat. There's a storm coming.

MJ Kobernus, Norway, 2018

Chapter 1 – The Storm

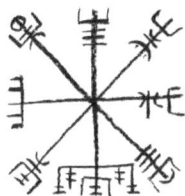

"There is peace, even in the storm."
~ Vincent Van Gogh

The storm hit the cove like a sledgehammer. As one, a dozen boats swung around, their bows pointing into the onslaught. A small sloop pulled hard on her anchor line, and for a moment it looked like the 31 foot sailboat would drag. Then all backward motion stopped and she steadied, held fast by the heavy steel anchor dug deep in the Chesapeake Bay mud.

Onboard the sloop Delphinus, I crouched on one knee, face turned away from the ferocious wind. Was it thirty knots? Forty? From the look of the spray flying up from water it could be more, possibly even fifty knots. Where in hell had it come from?

With one hand I gripped the forestay, the other clutched a small hand axe. That little hatchet gave me a sense of being in control. Even in the face of the mounting storm, I felt that I had options. If the boat dragged, things could get tricky, but I could use the axe to sever the anchor line and then use the motor. *If* we dragged.

I studied the tree line, picking out one landmark, then another. A series of quick glances between them, head swinging, using their fixed points and I could gauge if the boat was moving. Satisfied that we were anchored fast, I stepped over to the mast and slipped the hatchet into a receptacle usually reserved for a winch handle.

I grinned. As the wind whipped my face with cold spray I stared straight into the rolling black clouds illuminated by occasional flashes of lightning. I admit it. I was exhilarated, thrilled. *This* was adventure.

A slight rocking and a change in the boat's balance informed me that my wife had come topside.

I turned and waved. Kate crouched behind the sprayhood and shouted something, but her words were snatched away. I made my way aft, in my mind the seaman's mantra playing on a loop: *One hand for yourself and one for the boat.*

I grabbed a rail on the coach roof, then reached for a shroud as I navigated the narrow side deck back to the cockpit.

"Do you want some coffee?" Kate raised a hand to her face, shielding her eyes which widened as she took in the frothing water all around us. I laughed and shook my head.

"No thanks, I'm fine. How are the kids?"

"They're sleeping. Let me know if you need anything." She glanced about the cove once again, watching the mess of boats fighting nature's fury as the wind pulled her honey blonde hair in all directions. She tried to capture the flailing strands, but it was no use. Then she ducked down into the cabin, pulling the companionway cover into place with a thump, sealing herself and our two daughters inside where it was warm and dry. I did not regret that I had to stay on deck; I was loving it.

We had no idea it was going to be like this when we set out earlier that day. The storm front had come out of nowhere, and we were clearly not the only ones to be surprised by it. When we arrived in the late afternoon, it had been a very different scene indeed.

Shaped roughly like a horseshoe, the cove was both sheltered and beautiful. Many cruising boats had sought it out, most arriving before sunset in order to have time to drop anchor, prepare food, and appreciate the lush autumn colors before dark set in.

The russet and gold tones of the trees surrounding the small bay like a thick blanket did not disappoint. From the water's edge and up the broad hillside, a stunning tapestry of color and form rippled and danced in the light breeze.

We entered this little wonderland before dusk. There were already a number of sailboats and smaller motorboats resident when we picked our spot and dropped anchor but we had good space to swing and were not in anyone's way.

As the sun disappeared behind the trees, a large motorboat arrived. An older Chris-Craft, at least a forty-footer, it weaved its way between the sailboats heading close to shore and skinny water.

They dropped anchor and when the motorboat's engines finally cut out, silence reigned supreme. Only the whine of mosquitoes intruded on our peace.

But on the newly arrived motorboat there was a flurry of activity. Something big and black was pushed into position on deck. Then a generator kicked into operation and a bass heavy riff filled the air. Like a magnet, smaller boats were drawn to the Chris-Craft, tying themselves off alongside. They had obviously been waiting for it to arrive. Music pumped and people climbed aboard. Within minutes, the cove had gone from serene tranquility to a frat party.

The noise travelled easily over the water. Close to the inlet, I had been taking my ease in the cockpit. But as the speakers flooded the anchorage with noise, I stood and shook my head. Then, with a wry smile, I stooped, leaning over the open hatch of the companionway.

"So much for a quiet night then," I said.

Kate responded in the peculiar way Norwegians have, with a sharp intake of breath, which in this context meant, 'Yes, but what can you do?' She proceeded to put our oldest daughter to bed in the starboard quarter berth. The youngest was already asleep on the port side. The quarter berths were perfect for them, needing only to be secured by netting across the relatively small openings. I had secured the netting with bungee cords, tied to brass pad-eyes. It was a simple solution to the problem of how to keep the kids safe in their bunks. They were a handful, those two. At six months, and two years of age respectively, they needed constant watching.

It had been a poor season for sailing so far. At least, for us. I had spent far too much time at work, plus the kids made it all the harder to go out. Preparing a liveaboard boat to actually sail takes a lot of time. Yet here we were, in what was supposed to be a cruisers' paradise. But while the view had not changed, the noise was now prodigious. Aside from raising the anchor and moving on, there was not much we could do about the situation. And frankly, I did not like the idea of night sailing. We had only paper charts, not being able to afford a Garmin or similar GPS map system and I was far from confident in my abilities. There was a reason that we passed a lighthouse on our way here, after all.

"Could be worse," I said. Kate did not respond, busy as she was. I looked back towards the shore. At least the party boat was on the other side of the cove. It did not help all that much, but it was something.

Several sailboats, much closer to the Chris-Craft,

had become busy themselves, with clearly irate skippers on deck protesting the noise with crossed arms, scowls, and in once case a comically shaken fist.

I pulled the hatch cover back into position to keep the mosquitoes out and stood looking out at the bay, one hand on the boom. There is no getting around the fact that I am a big man and Delphinus is small, so I am always careful to hold onto something. Even though we were stationary and the water was like glass, I did not wish to trip over my own feet and take a dive. The Chesapeake in late Fall is cold.

Footsteps sounded below, then the companionway hatch slid back. Kate looked up at me, worry lines creasing her forehead.

"There's a storm warning," she said.

"What?"

"A storm is moving in. It's on the radio."

The VHF. We had left it on, just in case. We always did that, but this was the first time it had proven useful, other than for chatting to friends on other boats. I looked to the sky. It was twilight, and the sun had just disappeared behind the trees, so there was still light, but there was simply no indication of heavy weather.

"You sure?"

"That's what they said."

"How long?"

She shrugged. "I don't know."

"Okay. Could you pass me my jacket, please? I'll stay topside, just in case." I turned away, paused, then looked back. "And see if you can find the axe."

That had been an hour ago. Now the storm was upon us in full force. Still on the foredeck, I checked my landmarks again and still Delphinus had not dragged. We were doing okay, and I felt a little bit of pride. I was not an experienced sailor, and it gave me a fair bit of satisfaction to know that we had anchored well, in spite of the wind, which continued unabated. If anything, it was even stronger. Above the howling gale, the rhythmic thumping bass from the motorboat provided a musical counterpoint. I turned my head slightly. Was it getting louder?

It was. The raft of boats tied to the Chris-Craft were dragging. They had set only one anchor before the storm and that was obviously not enough. As I squinted into the spray, there was no mistaking their destination; they were heading directly for us.

I checked to see if the axe was still there, then I settled myself on the coach roof, face turned slightly away from the stinging wind and water, one eye on the boats drifting inexorably in our direction.

Other boats were dragging too and several had crossed each other, tangling anchor lines. Their owners desperately tried to separate themselves. I watched as two small sailboats, already entwined, were blown directly towards a third, a much larger Beneteau. Securely anchored, the big sailboat was powerless to stop the other two from colliding with it.

The captain hurriedly tied fenders over the port side. The drifting boats collided with the Beneteau and I winced in sympathy. Then there was a flurry of motion as their crews tried to push them apart, but to no avail. Something must have snagged. They had become one unit, hanging on the Beneteau's anchor.

Was it was better to cut our own anchor line and use the engine to avoid the same thing happening to us? Maybe, but not yet. We did not have a very powerful engine, so it would be a last resort.

Amazingly, the trio of boats did not drag. Even the captain of the Beneteau seemed surprised. I gave them a thumbs up, but no one noticed. A quick glance back at my landmarks; still no change. I looked back to the party boat. It was considerably closer. Two of its satellite boats had now removed themselves and were trying to set their own anchors. Thankfully, it was not very deep in the cove, so a long rode was not necessary, but they were close enough that if the wind shifted they would clearly cross each other's lines. I guess that was a risk they were willing to take. I could not blame them.

But the party boat was getting too close for comfort so I went back to the cockpit. With one hand I gripped a stay, then a handrail, then the sprayhood. Once safely in the protection of the cockpit, I started the auxiliary engine. It fired up immediately. I left it in neutral, and it idled with the regular thump-thump of a single cylinder diesel. Then I made my way forward again, never once forgetting my mantra. Retrieving the axe, I knelt by the anchor line and waited. If those boats came any closer, I would hack the anchor free and try to motor out of harm's way.

I did not like the idea of losing the anchor. They were not cheap. Hopefully we would be able to retrieve it in the morning, but its loss would be a small price to pay to avoid an insurance claim, or worse.

The skipper of the party boat had managed to get a dinghy in the water. Some crewmen were kedging out an anchor from the stern. They rolled a big anchor over the side, then turned and made their way back.

I watched keenly as the skipper of the Chris-Craft snubbed off the second anchor. For a moment, the boat continued its downwind drift then it swung about, swinging gently. The anchor was holding.

The party boat had stopped not more than fifteen feet away from Delphinus. Inside the cabin on the Chris-Craft, young men and women still danced and laughed, oblivious to the drama all around them.

I laughed too. It looked like I would not need the axe after all. The party boat captain made his way aft and called out to me, but the music and the wind were too loud. He looked young, no more than twenty-five. I raised a hand, a gesture meant to convey hello and relief that we were not more intimately acquainted.

He shrugged as if to say, what can you do? Stooping he retrieved something from a cooler on the deck then tossed it towards me. I leaned out over the push pit and snatched a can from the air; Coors.

I smiled even wider and popped the can, raising it in salute to the other skipper who also now held a beer aloft. The music was loud, the beer was cold and the wind was howling. Was this sailing? It was not what I had expected, but I would take it over a nine-to-five job, any day.

Chapter 2 – Learning to be Free

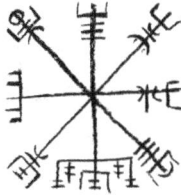

"Life is really simple, but we insist on making it complicated."

~ Confucius

That storm was over twenty years ago. My little sailboat, Delphinus, has been gone almost as long, as has Kate, come to mention it. Truth be told, that was not her real name. But for privacy's sake, when talking about real people, I have changed one or two things to allow for plausible deniability.

I have often wondered where my old boat is, and who is sailing her. Over the years, I would frequently think about tracking her down and maybe buying her back, but occasional searches of the Internet failed to reveal her location, so eventually I gave up. At least, I gave up looking, but I have never forgotten her.

Delphinus was a Seafarer 31. Seafarer is not a particularly famous or prestigious marque, but she was well built, with good lines and could handle gale force winds with aplomb.

She came from Huntington, New York originally. Commissioned in 1976, her designers were McCurdy and Rhodes. Seafarer Yachts put out a good many boats of varying (some might say questionable) quality, but I think they did a very good job with Delphinus. She had a luxurious teak and mahogany interior and a chart table to die for. Clearly, she had been kitted out with offshore racing in mind and no expense had been spared. In fact, there was talk of the boat being sailed by one of the owners of the company, but I do not know if that was true.

Whatever the case, she was my first boat so there will always be a special place for her in my heart. Of course, there have been others since then, but like they say about love and sex, you never forget your first.

There is another saying that I should mention, particularly when it comes to boats. It is, 'the two happiest days in a sailor's life are the day he buys a boat, and the day he sells it.' That is, I can tell you, simply nonsense.

I was forced to sell Delphinus and it was not an easy decision to make. Circumstances demanded it, and to paraphrase Shakespeare's apothecary, it was my poverty and not my desire that consented.

It is not merely nostalgia that makes me regret my decision to let her go. Sure, I had some good times on that boat. But far more importantly, Delphinus represented something vital to me, something above and beyond just being my home.

Without wishing to be overly dramatic, I think that the boat answered a need in my soul. Without it, I had a feeling that something fundamental was missing. That boat was an essential part of me, like an arm or a hand, and I felt its loss keenly.

As I said, it was more than just a boat. It represented a way of life that I desperately wanted. It meant freedom, adventure and most importantly, *living life on my own terms.*

This last sentiment was something that had

covertly nagged me for years. Even before I could understand it I felt a need to explore, to travel and to do anything that I was expressly told not to do. I was a contrarian, and still am. Like James Dean, I wanted to rebel. I just didn't understand why. I was a rebel without a clue.

I became aware of this peculiar condition when I was a young man, although at the time I could not articulate it or explain it very well and I certainly did not understand it. But as I got older, I became acutely conscious of a desire to live a different life than that of my family or my friends.

In time, this desire would be responsible for my making some crazy decisions. Still, as the song says, 'je ne regrette rien.'

Interlude, July 1989

I squinted into the impossibly bright sun, then looked quickly away. Italy in August is too hot. But what did I expect? The country is famous for its good weather.

I adjusted my ill-fitting backpack and headed into the noisy throng crowding the train station and examined the signs above the platforms. I had never been in Naples before but I have a knack for looking like I belong. The secret? Walk fast and act like you know where you are going.

There were a good many tourists, and most of them looked lost. In spite of the fact that I was not really sure where to go, I strode purposefully, weaving between the elegant Neapolitans standing around high tables with tiny cups of cappuccino, Africans carrying sacks full of knock-off handbags, a crowd of Koreans (none less than a hundred years old) and the inevitably ubiquitous Australians who seemed to delight in comparing everything to their homeland.

"Not very big, is it Bruce?" said one, with a nod indicating the station.

"Nah," replied the diminutive Bruce. "Central is much bigger."

I passed them with a smile. Central station in Sydney may be physically larger, but it handles a fraction of the number of passengers. A four to one difference in favor of the Italian station.

I squeezed past them, trying not to knock into anyone with my rucksack. I looked forward to getting on my train, so I could dump the bag. My shoulders hurt where the straps cut into them and no matter how I tried to shift the weight into a comfortable position it was hopeless. The backpack was Russian military, made from heavy canvas, circa 1950. Clearly it had been designed by a sadist, and I, obviously a closet masochist, had bought it. Well, it was too late for regrets. I was in Italy, I was about to board a train for the southern tip of the country and I was on a mission. A little discomfort was nothing given what I was about to do.

If you visualize the shape of Italy, it looks awfully like a boot (albeit one with a high stiletto heel). The area I was heading to was Reggio Calabria, and can be found on the 'toe.' I did not know much about Calabria, or the tiny town whose name was printed on the postcard residing in my wallet. This postcard was the reason I was there. I had received it a week prior and it finally answered the question of where my friend Selena had gone. All I knew was that she was in Italy. What and how she was doing were simply mysteries.

But mysteries now answered. The postcard showed a large hotel on a beach, with its name printed above. In blue ink, there was an arrow drawn, pointing to a window. On the back of the card was a hastily scrawled note. "Settling in. working as sous chef. You can see my room at the top. Weather is lovely. Wish you were here."

It was not an invitation. Just a 'letting you know how I am' type of postcard. Even the last part, "wish you were here" was clearly formulaic. Like, "Get well soon" on a card for someone in the hospital. After all, what else can you say?

No, it was most certainly not an invitation. But I had missed my chance to hell her how I felt about her before she left. Something had held me back. Was it cowardice? I like to think that the right opportunity never came up but that is hogwash. How hard is it to say, "By the way, I love you. Romantically, I mean."

Regardless of my excuse, my best friend left without knowing how I felt about her and I wanted to remedy that.

Now that I had an address of sorts, I made a plan to visit. I withdrew my meager savings from the bank, bought a ticket to Naples and waited impatiently for the day of the flight. I was going to finally tell her how I felt and to hell with the consequences. I was done with the 'friend zone.'

However, that moment was still a full day away, as I had to travel half the length of the country on a train that I was sure I could outrun over a short distance. Nonetheless, once I had found the right carriage (second class) I was happy to relax on the surprisingly well-sprung seats.

Before long, the compartment began to fill. Two female backpackers, all blond hair, blue eyes and flashing smiles joined me. From the flag pins on their backpacks I deduced they were Finnish. Then a pair of nuns arrived, one young, the other very old. I wondered if they always traveled in such pairs.

The younger nun helped the elder to sit. Arthritis

was obviously troubling the senior nun. Once seated, she gave me a nod and a brief smile. The younger nun seated herself, and immediately both ladies proceeded to worry their rosary beads. I wondered if that might be why the older woman had problems with her hands. Was carpal tunnel syndrome a common problem for nuns?

Inside the carriage it was shady but far from cool. The window was open but there was no breeze so we instinctively created a still life, everyone motionless. One of the backpackers foolishly attempted to fan herself with a folded map but soon gave it up as the effort clearly outweighed any benefit.

Then the train lurched, stopped, lurched again and began slowly to pull out of the station. I breathed a deep sigh as a slight breeze found its way inside and teased my sticky skin. As warm as I was, surely it was worse for the nuns as they were dressed in layers of heavy cotton. However, it quickly became apparent that they were used to the heat. Only the Finnish girls and I seemed to be bothered. I looked up and caught one's attention.

"Hot," I said, by way of introduction.

The girl seated nearest the window gave me a brief smile and nodded. "Yeah."

And that was it. We fell into silence again. I stared listlessly out of the window, watching the parched tan and brown scenery roll slowly past. After maybe thirty minutes into our eight-hour journey, the younger nun spoke.

"Where is everyone going?"

Her English was heavily accented, but perfectly understandable. The Finnish girls responded with a name I did not know. I answered with Calabria.

"Oh, where in Calabria?" the young nun requested, one eyebrow slightly raised.

I fished my wallet out of my pocket, extracted the postcard from Selena and passed it over. She looked at it, then frowned. Turning to the older nun, they proceeded to converse very quickly in Italian. Naturally, I did not understand a single word. Then the older nun shrugged, said something emphatic and went back to her beads.

"I think," said the younger nun, "that you cannot get off the train there."

"Sorry? What do you mean?"

"The train will not stop. There is a station, maybe forty kilometers past this place. You will have to get a taxi or wait for the bus in the morning."

We would be arriving in late evening, and it seemed that the only bus would go about nine in the morning. I sighed. I would just have to sleep on the bus stop, since I could not possibly afford to take a taxi back to the hotel. But perhaps there was another way? I spied the conductor making his way down the passage outside our compartment. I leaped up, and asked in carefully enunciated English, as if speaking to a child, if indeed the train did not stop at my destination. He looked at my postcard and nodded, adding a very Italian shrug as apology.

It was too much. I had come too far to overshoot by forty kilometers. There had to be another way!

The conductor checked our tickets and turned to leave, but I was not done with him. I addressed the young nun.

"Excuse me. Can you ask him if they will stop the train, so I can get off there?"

She asked. The answer was no. Perhaps I looked stricken, because she launched into a speech. The conductor looked at her, then looked at me and shrugged. But then he spoke again and the nun nodded. The conductor left, moving on down the train to the next carriage.

"They are not allowed to stop. But they will slow the train near the town. It is on a bend, so it goes slowly anyway. They will slow it more and you can simply jump off."

I was astounded! Jump from a moving train? But it was either that, or wait a whole night for a bus. I bit my lip, considered my options and figured what the hell! It seemed like the only logical thing to do.

Italians are a warm people and understand love and how it can make you do crazy things. Apparently, jumping from a moving train is reasonable when love is on the line. Who was I to argue? Besides, they said the train would be going slow. Looking out the window at the now flashing scenery, I thought that it would have to slow down a very great deal to tempt me to step off of it.

For much of the rest of the journey we rode in silence. The Finns eventually left and a couple of young men in soldier's uniforms took their seats. And then the conductor returned and motioned for me to follow him.

I grabbed my bag. The older nun gave me a blessing (I assume it was a blessing. It could just as easily have been last rites.) Then the young nun, the soldiers and the conductor all accompanied me to the carriage door, which the conductor had already opened. The bend in the track was approaching and the train was slowing with a squeal of brakes. It still seemed awfully fast.

But there was no time to think, no time to reconsider. The conductor took my rucksack and tossed it out the door. It rolled down the bank in a cloud of dust. He slapped me on the back and with my heart in my throat, I stepped out. Then I was rolling down the bank, ending up entwined in a scraggly bush. I was not winded, which surprised me. I stood up and waved to show I was okay. The nun waved back, then the door was pulled closed. Numerous faces looked out in surprise as another half dozen carriages clattered past slowly.

It could not have been going much more than fifteen miles an hour when I jumped out, and the train started to pick up speed immediately. I walked back to my bag, hoisted it on my shoulder and began to follow the tracks. They would take me into town and to Selena.

* * *

For me, this story illustrates a willingness to 'roll the dice' and to take a chance. Something that I believe is a very real part of sailing. However, while mitigating risk is something that one strives to do when sailing, there is no question that it *is* a risky way of life and you have to be willing to accept that. Of course, that was still far in my future, but I think that even in my early twenties, I was learning that one cannot live life in a bubble of safety or security. At least, I could not.

I am not saying that I would seek out risky situations. For example, I was never one for extreme sports. Those people that free climb on buildings without a harness and then dangle themselves from insane heights by just their finger tips are idiots. Life is too precious to risk just for kicks.

But I had no problem in riding a motorcycle year after year, crisscrossing Europe and risking the hazards of the road. Experience had taught me what to look out for when riding in traffic. I do not think it is a sixth sense, but I could always tell which drivers were more likely to be clueless and would change lanes without warning. I knew better than to stay inside a driver's blind spot, and I was always more alert at on and off ramps and junctions. While riding a motorcycle can never be as safe as driving a car, if you learn to ride defensively, you reduce your risk. In over thirty years of riding bikes, I have had a grand total of two accidents and both were my fault. The first was when I was a newly minted rider on my little 50cc Yamaha. I took a bend too fast and skidded on gravel. The second occurred about twenty-five years later, when I was driving in rush hour traffic and hustling to get home quickly. When the cars all came to a screeching stop, I braked hard and locked up the front wheel resulting in a spill.

In neither situation was I severely hurt. My ego may have been more bruised than my bottom. But these falls were a warning to always think, always be alert and always be ready for the unexpected. Lessons that I took to heart and tried to apply aboard boats, just as much as on two wheels.

And should you be wondering just what happened after I told Selena how I felt, well, I think you can guess. Inevitably, she rejected my suit and left me heartbroken. Anyone with an ounce of sense could have seen that coming. I returned to England a little more tanned and a little wiser.

Back then I had a restless spirit and I reveled in it. Years later that restless spirit would cause me to refuse a pay raise and give up my job so that I could drive my family across half the US in order to live in a sailboat.

Perhaps I am a little impulsive. However, I have never regretted anything that I have done. As they say, it is better to regret what you did, than regret what you didn't. And while I was young and single, this was easy. There was only myself to consider and I had no duty or obligation to think about anyone else.

Of course, when I became a family man, this became much harder. When one has a family, it is *their* needs that come first. Striking a balance between obligation and self-interest is a challenge, and one I have been wrestling with for decades.

Although I was born in Cook County, Illinois, I actually grew up in England. This will partly explain the fusion of US and UK English that you will no doubt notice while reading this book. And it will also explain why many anecdotes appear to be Brit centric.

When I was fifteen, I got my first job in order to save for a motorcycle. Bikes were all I dreamed of back then, and I could identify a motorcycle merely from the sound of its engine or the shape of its brake light.

My family lived well below the poverty line. We were poor and there was no such thing as 'pocket money' or an allowance, let alone enough money for a motorbike. But some instinct informed me that a bike was all I needed to be happy. I was determined to do whatever it took to get one.

This was the first time I had ever set myself a major goal, and I worked hard, saving every penny I made. Finally, the time came when I had scraped together enough money to purchase my first bike and I was ready to join the local 'gang,' the group of kids around my age lucky enough to have our own wheels.

We used our bikes to explore the countryside, and I developed an appreciation of the twisting English 'B' roads at that time. We traveled surprisingly far on our little machines, not minding that they only did 30-35 miles per hour (about 50-55 kilometers).

We would lie over the tanks to minimize windage, but that did not really help. We just got used to riding for hours on end, the little engines buzzing like so many angry bees.

I did not take any lessons before getting on the bike. I learned through trial and error (as I would later do with sailing). And yes, I fell off once in the most spectacular way. But that was a lesson I needed to learn! Gravel rash is a particularly effective teacher. *I do not recommend it.*

Since those halcyon days on my Yamaha I have been infatuated with all kinds of motorcycles. As infatuated as I later became with sailboats. And, strange as it may seem, I believe that the reasons for my obsession for bike and boat stem from exactly the same source.

There is a part of me that does not feel 'whole' unless I have a motorcycle. Even if I do not use my bike much, just knowing it is there gives me a sense of peace.

As I write this, I have a 1975 Honda GL1000 standing in the garage, looking glorious. And although I drive a car to the office most days, I catch a glimpse of the bike every morning and every evening, and I know that if I wanted to I could get on that bike and just ride. I could go anywhere and do anything. I would not be restricted by traffic jams or road barriers. *I would be free.*

The idea that a penniless teenager with practically zero education could ever truly be free to live life on his own terms might be illusory but it is what drove me when I was fifteen and it is what still drives me now, more than 35 years later.

I guess it all comes down to having anti-social attitudes. For example, I preferred karate to football and reading to partying. As a teen, I was aware of this tendency to isolate myself, but I did not think it a bad thing. On the contrary, while my friends were out throwing stones at factory windows, I was in the library studying history. To me, casual vandalism was pointless, while understanding the hundred year's war was highly interesting.

Clearly, I was willing to reject conventional lifestyle choices, even in my teens. In spite of this, I had no clue where I wanted my life to go. I was certainly not interested in sailing back then. The only thing boating related that caught my attention were reports on *Morning Cloud,* the sailing yacht owned by the former British Prime Minister, Ted Heath. I can distinctly recall watching the news coverage of the 1979 Fastnet race, where *Morning Cloud* failed to finish due to a lost rudder.

At that time, sailing did not have any hold on me, and I was aware of it in only the most abstract of ways. It was as remote from my life as undersea exploration or spaceflight.

So what was it that drew me to the sea, so many years later? Was it the books that I had read? At thirteen, I lost myself in Ted Simon's *Jupiter Travel's,* and I immediately began to plan my own motorcycle journey around the world (something I still dream about). This then led me to read books by other travelers and explorers. I read Heyerdahl's book on the Kon-Tiki expedition and Aku-Aku, his book about Easter Island, and I fantasized about going there one day and seeing the giant moai for myself.

When I read Heyerdahl's books on the Ra expeditions, where he built a great raft and attempted to sail across the Atlantic, I was intrigued, but at no point did I contemplate building my own, home grown boat from willows and reeds.

So what was it that finally brought me to the realization that boats are the ultimate mode of transport? I really have no idea, except perhaps an innate frugality. After all, the wind is free.

Whatever it was, I intuitively understood that the

sense of freedom that I had loved with motorcycles was exactly the same with a sailboat. I was struck with the glorious knowledge that, should I wish, I could take a boat anywhere I truly wanted to go in the world. That is a very powerful realization.

There is a great sense of peace knowing that you are not tied down to one place because of rules or obligations, but rather through choice. And should you choose to leave, nothing can stop you.

The idea of freedom, even if it is mostly a delusion, was a critical part of what brought me to motorcycles, and then later to sailing. Freedom is a powerful sentiment, and I felt it calling out to me; a siren song pulling me towards the sea.

But in spite of the fact that one is never very far from water in England, I did not get a boat there. In fact, it had not yet occurred to me that I could. Both Kate and I had just finished University, and we had just had our first child.

Yes, in spite of the fact that I left school with no qualifications, I had blagged my way into University by impressing the interviewing professor. The night before I visited the hallowed halls of Birmingham University, I had stayed up to watch a Star Trek movie on TV; the 'Wrath of Khan.'

In one of the final scenes, Khan tells Kirk that he would rather rule in Hell than serve in Heaven. Later, Spock asks Kirk about that and Kirk informs him that it is a quote from Milton's 'Paradise Lost.'

This stuck in my mind, and the next day when I asked the professor about the reading curriculum, he mentioned Milton.

"Ahh," I said. "Better to rule in Hell than to serve in Heaven."

The professor was delighted that one of his potential students could so easily quote Milton, his particular passion and area of expertise. I got an offer from the University, including some financial support. Quite a stroke of luck for someone that had never heard of Milton before. Just one more reason that I have to be grateful to Star Trek.

Three years later and I graduated with honors. Then I went on to do some post grad studies. But now, with our academic life coming to an end, I saw an opportunity to do something different. It would mean selling my beloved bike, a Yamaha XJ900, but it would be worth it. We were leaving England for good.

But if the grass was not actually any greener on the other side, then at least it would be a little different. As were many things, I was soon to discover.

Chapter 3 – Puddle Jumping

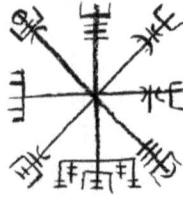

"The most important thing in life is to stop saying I
wish, and start saying I will."

~ *Charles Dickens*

We decided that it was time to experience America,
my nominal homeland, and we made plans to relocate
to Chicago.

That period of my life was full of firsts. Two weeks
after our daughter's birth, I flew to Chicago, and
started the process of looking for work and getting a
place to live.

I quickly found both, and soon enough I managed
to convince a bank to lend me enough money to buy a
two-bedroom condo in River Forest, a relatively
upscale suburb of the Windy City.

It is a grand and exciting thing to move from one
country to another and I was kept busy with
discovering new aspects of life in the US, including
open all-night diners, drive through banking and all
you can eat buffets (the last of which is the bane of my
existence).

However, about six months after moving, I began
to feel that something was wrong with my new life. I
knew myself well enough by then to know what was
missing and a quick scan of the classifieds told me

that what I needed was easily available.

It was a typical midweek evening in our apartment. Our daughter was asleep in her bedroom, I had a book open and the smell of a frozen pizza cooking in the oven filled the room. I looked up at Kate who was sitting on the other end of the sofa.

"I think I'll get another bike," I said.

Kate lowered the magazine she had been reading, regarded me with one eyebrow slightly arched, then said, "Pardon?"

"I said, I think I'll get another bike."

She contorted her face into an expression that would have been appropriate if I had mentioned that I wanted to drink bleach.

"Are you mad?" She exclaimed. "You can't have a bike. What about the baby?"

I knew what she was getting at, and I had wrestled with the question many times, but I wanted to be obtuse.

"I'm sure they have really small helmets for kids," I replied, trying to suppress a smile.

This conversation quickly devolved into an argument about responsibility, life insurance, raising a child as a single mother (and a widow, to boot) and my not caring about them.

Strange how, before our first child came along, we had both loved motorcycles. In fact, we had driven all over Europe together. In one memorable trip, we went from Krakow Poland, to Birmingham, UK in a single 24-hour period, a distance of approximately 1,150 miles, or 1,850 kilometers. We were hardcore bikers. Neither snow nor rain nor heat nor gloom of night could stop us from . . . Wait, isn't that the Postal Service?

Yet now it seemed that my desire to get another motorcycle was as ridiculous as stating that I wanted to live on the Moon.

It is one of the most predictable outcomes of having a baby that the motorcycle must go. If you are lucky and your wife loves you, then you might get another when the kids have graduated college.

While I can understand the motivation for this demand, I did not like it. It seemed both cruel and unfair that I could not have what I wanted, while Kate got exactly what she needed from life. I wanted to rail against the inequality of it. I wanted to demand my rights as the man, the head of the house and the breadwinner.

Needless to say, I did not get another motorcycle. This was partly prompted by a near death experience with a 16-year-old and his father's BMW that occurred just weeks later. The youngster came out of a side alley at speed and crashed his car into mine, causing me to spin out of control, narrowly avoiding being crushed by a large dump truck driving in the opposite direction.

Kate's response to this event was to suggest that I buy a tank and obviously I could forget about a motorcycle for the rest of my life. I wanted to assert my independence and get a bike anyway, but instead I opted for an SUV which, no matter how hard I tried to convince myself, is not almost as good.

And, as much as I loved feeling like the king of the road in my gas guzzling truck, it did not afford me the same sense of quiet freedom that a bike would have given me.

But I was a husband and a father, and I did what everyone in my position does; I went to work and tried to forget about what I really wanted.

Kate demanded five years to be at home with our daughter while I worked to support them. I was not really in favor of this, although I could not argue that it was best for our little girl. But I was concerned that we could not afford such a luxury. We were not wealthy. Far from it! In England we had been penniless students. And now, in the US, we were perennially penniless immigrants.

We barely had enough money to pay our bills, so I felt it was an 'all hands on deck' situation. But Kate stuck to her guns, insisting that she stay home. I buckled on that decision too.

Prior to going to college, I had been very much a blue-collar worker. In fact, I left school without a diploma or any kind of qualifications. For just over a decade, I worked at hard, manual jobs that often demanded both unsociable hours and a willingness to tolerate dangerous conditions. I had been a baker for six years, worked on a building site for a year, driven a heavy goods truck for a year, worked on a psych ward, and then later worked with mentally handicapped adults in both a hospital and a group home for over two years.

And while I had not done well in school, that did not mean that I was not smart, nor well read. In fact, I have always believed that one should not allow one's schooling to get in the way of one's education.

As I said previously, I went to Birmingham University where I found that my life experience gave me a distinct advantage over newly minted high school graduates.

Ultimately, I left with a good degree and a plan to leverage my education into something a bit more upscale, even, dare I say it, white collar.

A measure of my desperation to succeed can be seen in just what I was willing to put up with. My first real job was for a retail giant, who shall remain nameless. They were big, well known, and had stores in every contiguous state of the US.

I thought that they would be a good, secure and safe bet. They had the façade of stability, which, as it turns out, really was a façade. They were in chapter 13 when I joined, and were heading for bankruptcy without passing GO and without collecting 200 dollars.

I think it is strange that no one mentioned that pertinent fact when I applied for the position of Quality Assurance Analyst. I went for an interview at the corporate headquarters in the near north side of downtown Chicago. After it concluded, one of the interviewers took me aside for a quiet word, and in all seriousness said the following:

"You seem like a nice guy. Do yourself a favor. If you get an offer, don't accept it. You don't want to work here."

I did not know what to say, so I simply nodded and took my leave. But I was not in a position to be picky. Our savings were gone and I needed a regular gig, post-haste. When I got a phone call later that day asking when I could start, I took the job.

I started the following Monday, and almost immediately understood why my new colleague had tried to warn me. Our boss was not quite as nice as he appeared during the interview.

I am not going to catalogue the daily indignities that were foisted upon us. I am sure there are many who suffer as badly, or worse, and still smile and put up with it. But the toxic environment caused by our boss' acute micro-managing and foul temper wore me down.

Every morning, when I awoke, I would feel good just for a moment. Then I would remember that I had to go to work and it would happen. A knot of tension would develop in my stomach, feeling like a ball of lead, pulling me down. And with every mile that I drove closer to my office, that knot of tension would become bigger and stronger.

I no longer felt like the king of the road in my SUV; instead, I felt like a sacrificial lamb going to the slaughterhouse. Even worse, I was driving myself!

I was now firmly part of the corporate machine, and I hated it. I hated my job, my boss and the people I worked with (there were a few notable exceptions.) In short, I was on the fast track to a heart attack, a nervous breakdown or going postal.

Was this what I had signed up for? Was this *my* dream? Obviously not. But I stuck it out. I was not doing it for myself, but for my family. It is amazing just how much shit a person can take when he or she knows there is a little kid waiting at home.

But there is a limit, and after eighteen months, I had reached mine. I began to look for ways to improve my situation.

Thoreau said that, "The mass of men lead lives of quiet desperation. What is called resignation is confirmed desperation." I understood that statement now far more than when I had first read it. It is a sobering and most unpleasant thought to know that it applies to oneself.

This was not the life that I had aspired to. But that would change, and fast. I do not remember the exact day that it happened or what triggered it. But like a proverbial bolt of lightning, I was suddenly struck with the realization that boats, like bikes, offered the same potential for freedom. Only a boat, let's be fair, allow you to travel the highways of the sea in considerably more comfort and style than a motorcycle ever could.

Without understanding why, I knew without doubt that my future lay with sailboats and sailing, with the wind and the sea.

What a revelation!

A motorcycle is good but a boat is better. After all, you can all travel together, there is plenty of room for the whole family, and no one needs to wear a helmet.

They say you can be 'bitten' by the sailing bug. I don't feel that this expression encompasses the enormity of what happened to me. I was not intrigued, or merely interested or curious. I was suddenly, overwhelmingly, completely and utterly *consumed* by all things boat related.

Perhaps if I had moved to a different job, then things might have been different. But I was fed up and I knew that another position with another company would not be enough.

I came to a very important realization. I was not merely looking for a better job. *I was looking for a better me.*

This was not something that I could easily explain, either then or now. I did not simply announce one day that I wanted to go on a spiritual pilgrimage, since I hardly knew it myself. All I knew, was that I had a condominium in a nice suburb of Chicago with a wife and baby daughter, a job that paid the bills and a big, shiny car but I was not, and this cannot be stressed enough, *happy.*

I have no doubt that this was in large part due to financial pressures. I now had car payments, a mortgage, insurance, cable and credit cards, to name but a few outgoings, and this entire house of cards was only supported by my willingness to eat shit.

There is a character in the movie 'Office Space' who complains that every day is worse than the one before, making every new day the worst of his life. This was something that I could sympathize with, as I too felt that each day was somehow worse than the preceding.

It was at this time that I really started to pile on the

pounds. Comfort eating is a cliché to which I subscribed in a major way. And while I was aware of my increasing girth, I seemed unable or unwilling to oppose it. I was more concerned with finding another job that would pay the bills but that did not require me to sacrifice my sanity or soul.

So I studied for Microsoft's various tech exams as a way to make myself more credible in the job market. To call me motivated would be an understatement.

I took my first exam on a Wednesday afternoon in downtown Chicago and I passed with flying colors. Encouraged, I dove into my studies and I took my seventh exam a mere six weeks later. I was now a qualified Microsoft Systems Engineer.

That looked great on my CV, which, frankly, was exactly what it was intended for. A paper MCSE is a computer engineer who has little or no practical experience, but has still passed the exams. That was me in a nutshell.

But moving to another job within the corporate world did not appeal to me. I knew intuitively that nothing would change except maybe the paint on the walls. Even if my boss was actually a decent human being, I would still be wasting my life in a cubicle, doing a job that meant nothing to me and for which I had no passion. It was not enough and I realized that I wanted more than just a change in environment: I wanted a fundamental change in lifestyle and most of all, I wanted to live a life of meaning. The only question that remained was, *how*?

Chapter 4 – The Plan

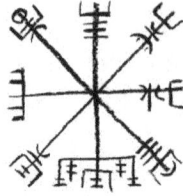

"God gave us the gift of life; it is up to us to give ourselves the gift of living well."

~ *Voltaire*

The realization that I was not living the life I wanted came to me one night in mid-October as I lay in bed. It was a genuine epiphany.

I suddenly *knew* with perfect clarity that I needed something quite different from the white picket fence, 2.4 children and a hyena that was considered the norm in polite society.

I wanted adventure and excitement. I wanted an outlet to all the creative energies that I felt bubbling up inside and I wanted to experience Nature directly, be more 'in touch' with things and maybe, just maybe, strike a balance between paying bills and *living*.

And that was the beginning of my obsession with things that float. I believed that living on a boat would enable me to finally grasp what I had been missing and what I believed that I needed to be happy. It would provide adventure and excitement and enable me to really be a part of the world, not just a cog in a corporate machine.

Many people have come to the same conclusion that I did. Some chose to buy a bus, or an RV. Others buy a plot of land in a remote area and build a simple cabin, going off-grid.

And while these approaches seem to me to be all equally fine, and I could probably embrace any one of them, for me the idea of using wind as a means of travel was just too appealing. It *had* to be a boat.

I started to buy magazines and trawl online catalogues. I studied marine architecture and tried to teach myself useful knots. I thought about taking sailing classes on Lake Michigan, but no one was going to teach me in the middle of winter. So I bought Chapman's and I read every page. Then I read it again, focusing on what I thought were the most important lessons for the newly inducted.

Kate was not impressed. Her idea of a good life involved parks and play dates and a husband who provided for the family.

I could not argue with that last sentiment, but I felt that there must be an alternative to allowing myself to be mentally and emotionally torn apart like so much meat in a grinder. We had a talk. I did not want to state my real reasons for wanting to 'drop out' since I was slightly ashamed of them, as if being unhappy with a job and being miserable were a sign of weakness. So, I thought it best to just jump straight into the topic and extoll its virtues. The sailing lifestyle, I was sure, would sell itself. The opportunity came one Sunday morning.

"How would you like to live on a boat?" I said.

"I wouldn't," Kate countered.

We were in downtown Oak Park, a charming town center of cafés and galleries. Having just had breakfast in our favorite diner, we were both at our most mellow. Kate pushed a stroller, while our daughter nodded off, happy and full after her silver dollar pancakes. I pulled my jacket closed to ward off the chill. It was a grim morning, with the sun barely showing itself. A perfect time to discuss sailing in warmer climes.

"I think it's something we should consider. We could move to the coast, buy a boat and go cruising. What could be better than that?"

We walked on a few more yards. Then Kate stopped. She was intrigued, but I could see she was far from persuaded.

"What are we going to do about money?"

The question was not irrelevant. It is the magical barrier that stops us from doing many things. But I already had an answer to that.

"Well, obviously I can get a job in IT pretty much anywhere now. I have all those Microsoft exams under my belt. They'll get my foot in the door and I can do the rest."

"What will I do?" Kate countered, her forehead creasing in puzzlement as she contemplated a future that involved living in a boat.

"What you do now. Look after the baby, look after the house, or rather the boat. I'll work, and in the weekends, we can go sailing."

"I don't know. I'll think about it."

Wisely, I did not press the issue. Kate would likely take a contrary position if she felt she was being pressured. We walked back to the car in silence. But I could tell she was mulling things over.

The seed had been planted. Now all it needed was a little water to help it grow. Surprisingly, help came from the most unlikely of places.

A few days later, I got a call in the middle of the night from my boss who needed me in the office pronto. I had recently been promoted to a new position, which, while it did not come with any extra money, came with a good deal of extra responsibilities, one of which was to oversee the distribution of software updates over an immense computer network.

The phone roused us from sleep and I grabbed it off the cradle. Without any preamble or apologies my boss came right to the point.

"Hey, Mike. I need you to come in right now."

I looked groggily at my watch. It was barely three o'clock in the morning. I struggled out of bed, still half asleep, mumbled something to my boss and tried to find my trousers.

Kate was angry, feeling that I was being taken advantage of, but I pointed out that I could not afford to make waves. I simply could not take the chance of being fired. Like many other families, we lived month to month, paycheck to paycheck. Since we had next to nothing in the bank, if I lost my job there was a very real possibility of losing our home as well.

For the first time, Kate realized how fragile our comfortable lifestyle really was. She had never really considered how important my job was, even though it underpinned everything. It was the single point of failure that could ruin us.

When I got back from work later that day I brought up the subject of buying a boat again. I had a good argument to win Kate over. We would own it outright and not owe anything to the bank, or anyone else. I would still work, but we could save, and in a year or two, go cruising. It would be an experience to remember for the rest of our lives and it would give our daughter the very best possible environment to grow up in. With both her parents at 'home' with her, and with so many wonderful experiences waiting, it was almost a crime *not* to do it.

To my immense gratitude, Kate agreed that she liked the idea and was willing to give it a try. I was ecstatic. Kate had more experience in sailing than I did (which for me was practically zero) and she had many fond memories of summer vacations sailing in Norway, where she had grown up. Even so, I was very surprised when she not only accepted the idea, but embraced it fully.

We were going to buy a boat, live on it, and learn to sail! We were going to *live the dream.*

Not having any savings, my first order of priority was to generate the cash with which to actually buy a boat. Since we did not have any investments or major assets to liquidate, we started small, selling off items of little value like books and table lamps.

Slowly our nest egg grew. But the process was far too slow for my liking and I organized a sale in the apartment. It was amazingly successful. At least fifty people came through during the half day we ran the open house and we got rid of a lot of stuff.

But once we were done reducing our clutter to the bare minimum, there was really just one asset that was worth more than everything else combined; our home, a charming little two-bedroom apartment in an Art Deco period building.

We put the condo up for sale. A local broker, the very same guy who had helped us buy it, now helped us sell it. With the apartment picked clean after our sale it had a rather Spartan look, but that just made it seem bigger.

We had it on the market for only a couple of weeks before we got an offer we could accept. After closing costs, what was left was enough to get us started. We had a grand total of about twenty-thousand dollars.

I felt rich, since I had arrived in the US with less than a grand, but of course, twenty-thousand is not a lot of money when you are talking about buying a boat, especially one big enough to comfortably live aboard. But it would do.

Once the sale was confirmed and earnest money had been paid into an escrow account, I gave two weeks' notice at work. My boss, bless his twisted evil little heart, did not want me to leave and offered me a substantial pay raise if I would stay. But money cannot buy happiness, (although I am told there are places in Vegas where you can rent it) and I declined without as much as a second's hesitation.

I told him, just as I told everyone at the office, what Kate and I were planning to do. The reactions to my announcement were polarized around two distinctly opposite opinions; I was either crazy or a genius. I like to think that the two are not mutually exclusive.

Many of my co-workers did not really believe it. Some would swing by my cubicle to question me about 'The Plan.'

These conversations often went the same way. One of my co-workers was Dan, an older guy from South Bend, Indiana. He was working out his 'sentence,' waiting to retire. He mulled the idea over as we sat and ate lunch together.

"Really? You're going to live in a boat?"

"Yep," I replied.

"What about school for your kid?"

"She's only a year old. Hardly an issue now."

"Yeah, I guess," he said, dubiously. "But what about health care?"

"We'll take our chances. I guess I can always get another job. And I can pay for insurance until then."

It had taken Dan over a year to find the position he now had. I could see he was skeptical.

"Might not be so easy to just walk into another job, right now," he added, authoritatively. "Look at the economy."

As far as I could see, the economy was fine, with the

lowest unemployment rate for years. Of course, from the perspective of his mid-fifties, he might be thinking about his own chances of finding another position. Since I was only in my early-thirties at that time, I felt that I had plenty of options.

I shrugged. "Well, we'll see. I'm doing it, and to hell with the consequences."

At that, Dan shot me a look of admiration (or so I like to think). He reached up to stroke his whiter than white colonel Sanders' beard.

"Wow. I have to say, I would love to do something like that. But not a boat. Never could stand the water. An RV. Yeah, that would be something. I would really love to get a Winnebago and hit the road."

He cast a furtive glance around, as if afraid that he had been overheard saying something shameful. No one was looking and he relaxed; his thought crime had gone unnoticed. I nodded encouragingly, and like any new convert, attempted to proselytize.

"You should. Just do it! You're never too old for a bit of adventure, right?"

He chuckled, then said, "Well, I don't know. I don't think my wife would go for it. Plus, when would I see my grandkids? Not to mention I have a mountain of debt."

Dan sighed and a haunted look came to his eyes. The same look that a Polar bear in the zoo has while it paces back and forth in its enclosure. Then he smiled wistfully. "But it sure does sound nice."

After lunch, we went back to our cubicles. Neither of us liked our office enclosures, but at least I was going to get out. I felt bad for Dan. He was a nice guy, trapped by financial constraints into doing a job he hated. He had ten years left before he would retire, and he counted down every day.

Dan was not the only one that thought my plans

both brave and foolhardy, yet wished me well for the future. Many of my co-workers claimed that they too would love to give up the rat race and 'drop out.' But no amount of encouragement or cajoling from my side could sway any them to actually do it. I began to wonder if they were institutionalized.

'Getting out' was clearly something that many dreamed of doing and paid lip service to, but they were not at all serious when it came down to it. There were always excuses and they seemed to be pretty much all the same. Debt. Money. Commitments. They were the same issues that I had wrestled with too, but I was determined not to let them hold me back.

Of course, not everyone was so enthusiastic about 'The Plan.' One friend declared that I would be living like a bum, an idea that amused me. As it turned out, his was the moderate position. Other people remarked on my recklessness. "You've got a kid. You have to be responsible" was a frequent refrain.

They even suggested that what I was doing was criminally negligent. I found it odd that so many people were vehemently against my wish to live life on my own terms. I did not judge them for their smoking and drinking or any number of other destructive habits. That was their business and this was mine.

I thought The Plan was brave, noble and adventurous. I was striving for a better way of life not just for myself, but for my family too. Naively, I believed that my example would spark a fire in their breasts and they would resign their hated jobs in order to follow their own dreams. Of course, that did not happen.

In fact, the reality was much sorrier, as I was to learn. A year later, I heard that Dan had died of a heart attack as he drove home from work.

I was shocked and saddened. Most of all, I was

sorry that Dan never achieved his dream of buying an RV and crisscrossing the US, seeing it all. He had waited too long to begin living his life, and in the end he simply ran out of time.

I was determined that I would not let the same thing happen to me. One way or another, I was going to get a boat, and make my dream a reality.

Chapter 5 – How to Afford a Boat

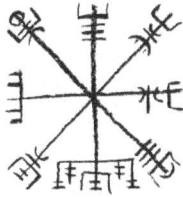

"The secret of happiness is not found in seeking more, but in developing the capacity to enjoy less."

~ *Socrates*

I am not an expert on finances. While not exactly hopeless, no one is rushing to give me a job on Wall Street, or even asking me to help with their taxes.

However, since finances are a vitally important topic and one which many people find challenging, I will relate just how simple buying a boat can be, if you are willing to be ruthless with yourself.

My approach to funding my first boat purchase was to apply a simple, if somewhat brutal, method. Stop spending.

Sounds easy, doesn't it? Well, it is and it isn't. You must eliminate every temptation to spend, no matter how small. There are so many things that we casually fritter money away on that we hardly think of it as spending at all. My approach was to treat any expense, be it large or small, with dread and fear. Nothing can be excused.

There are a million and one ways that money can be sucked from your bank account and your pocket, but you do not have to let it. Inspect your daily routine. Be honest. Where does it all go?

Are you tempted to buy a newspaper and a coffee to read on the train? Or how about a donut for a mid-morning snack? If you are, simply remind yourself of this one thing; every penny you spend is taking you further away from your dream.

I know it is hard to change the habits of a lifetime, but change you must (unless you are wealthy, in which case why are you reading this?) so the best thing is to just get on with it. Like ripping off a Band-Aid, there is no point in doing it a little at time. Jump in with both feet and do it.

If you have a full-time job, it might seem the height of folly to even consider giving it up. A regular pay check is something you can depend upon. It will enable you to achieve stability and security. It is a key part of planning one's future.

It is also, in some ways, an addiction. Not like heroin or even carbohydrates are an addiction. Nope, it is far more sinister.

Perhaps it is strange to imagine oneself being addicted to money, but we are. The fact is, we earn and spend a very great deal more than we actually *need*. We are wasteful and frivolous and sometimes downright reckless with our money.

I am sure that you have heard the expression, 'spending money like it was water.' This squandering of a finite resource should be tempered just as you would with any other resource. Money does not grow on trees, after all!

If you are anything like me, you will probably spend everything you earn (and just a little bit more) every single month. This is extremely dangerous and makes you vulnerable to any number of potential issues, from medical bills, sudden downsizing, car repairs, house repairs, and the list goes on.

Before I made the decision to buy a boat and move

aboard it, I found it impossible to save. Even when I changed jobs, got a pay raise and took home more money each week, I found that I spent more, so that any gain in income was immediately curtailed by my spending habits. Basically, no matter how much I made, I would spend it all. And no matter how much *your* income is, you may very well have the same issue.

This phenomenon is referred to as 'spending creep' and it affects a great many of us. To find out if you are prone to spending creep, try answering the following question.

When you get a little extra money do you,

A) Put it in a bank account you never touch
B) Take the family out to dinner?
C) Splash out on a new gadget?

This is not exactly a scientific survey! But, if you answered either B or C, you may very well be inclined towards spending creep.

Windfall money is perhaps the hardest not to spend. You might feel that you did not work hard for it, so why not blow it all? How about a trip to Vegas, or a new watch or some other luxury item that you could easily live without? After all, who amongst us has not bought something on an impulse that we really did not need?

It would seem that regardless of how much we earn, it is difficult to resist living beyond our means. However, in practical terms, if you analyze what you actually *need to live*, that is, how much money is required to obtain daily sustenance and basic shelter for yourself and your family, then the amount is shockingly little. So where does it all go?

A packet of gum here, a bottle of soda there, and suddenly you've burned through a couple of bucks. It all adds up.

Perhaps then, the addiction is not to money, per se, but rather to *spending*. Consider this:

You have probably heard the phrase, 'retail therapy.' While this was coined as a semi facetious term, I believe that for many it is a real problem. In fact, there is a scientific word for it; oniomania. No, it does not mean going crazy for onions (which I will admit I do) but rather a compulsion to shop, leading to negative consequences (typically debt, and huge credit card bills). This is sometimes referred to as 'Compulsive Buying Disorder,' and is often linked to other personality disorders, such as OCD and even Bipolarism.

There is a link between spending money and endorphins (those pesky opiates that make us happy) just as there is a link between endorphins and exercise, sex and many other activities.

Buying things, it would seem, makes some people temporarily happy. However, when they come down from that all too brief 'high' and start to feel a little sad and sorry, what do they do? Why, they just go out and buy another pair of shoes, or a phone or whatever it is that has caught their eye. It is a vicious circle that makes only shopkeepers happy.

If that sounds at all familiar, then you may well be addicted to spending.

When I was young and I wanted to buy something my mother would often say, "A penny saved, is a penny earned." I had no idea what that meant, but it must have had some impact on me, as I embraced 'making do' with a passion. Perhaps this story from my teenage years will help illustrate the point.

Interlude, June, 1980

I brushed the long unkempt hair out of my eyes, and nodded to my friend Brian as he mounted his bicycle. Even though Brian was now a skinhead and I was not, we were still friends. In fact, he was one of my oldest friends, someone I had known since I had first arrived with my family in England in 1972.

"See ya," I replied in response to his goodbye.

He waved and took off down the road, pedaling hard, quickly making progress as the rest of us kids not lucky enough to have a bicycle started to make our way home on foot.

It was unseasonably warm. With only a month to go before the end of term, the summer promised to be hot and long. Like every schoolkid, I was looking forward to it. Not because it meant the chance to be out playing all day long, but because it meant that I could get a job and save some real money.

Another friend had recently started working at the Saturday open air market, and he had recommended me for a job there. I was thrilled. Of course, it would mean getting up early, but I didn't care. I would have to be at the market around six in the morning to help set up a stall and unload a truck and then do anything else that was needed. I would be working on the fruit and veg stall.

Tomorrow would be my first day at my new job. It also meant I would get my first 'paycheck' too, something I looked forward to with excitement.

School was on the other side of town from where I lived and while it was not that far, it felt like a marathon trek. Two miles is not that much and I could get home in about fifteen minutes. So long as I did not dawdle.

I followed Castle Street, which is a longer, less direct route. Castle Street is a narrow, old road, going back many hundreds of years. It was named for the small castle that still stands there. Well, it was not really a castle. It is actually a Tudor country house.

I had snuck into the castle grounds in my younger days, only to be chased off by a gardener or game keeper. The castle is largely known for being the place where Henry VIII took Anne Boleyn in 1535 after their marriage. Of course, he had to chop the head off of its current owner (his cousin) before he could confiscate it. So much for noblesse oblige, but then King Henry was not known for being subtle!

It was not possible to see much of the castle from the road as it was set far back behind impressively tall chestnut trees. But the whole street displays its history at every turn, from the 12th century Norman church, to the many 17th century cottages to the tiny stone building that everyone said was the town jail.

The little stone building had not been used for years, but back in the day it was where people were held before being taken to the nearby city of Gloucester and tried. Tried, convicted and then hung, as was usually the case.

Like with the infamous Granny hanging of 1816, when a 69-year-old woman was condemned to death for stealing food from a neighbor. Her son was also found guilty, but he was lucky and his sentence was commuted to deportation, after which he was sent to Australia.

The descendants of that family still live in the town and everyone knows them. In fact, most of the world knows one of their cousins very well, as it is none other than Kylie Minogue.

Of course, I did not know about that connection at the time. Kylie would not become famous in the UK until 1986, with her role on a soap opera. I mention it because the town of Thornbury has precious few anecdotes of interest, in spite of the fact that it is very old, going back to at least 896 AD and probably much earlier than that.

I followed the semi cobbled road to the High Street. I did not mind walking. Most kids from school had to walk home. No one got picked up by car in those days and the school bus was only for those that lived far outside the town's borders. The only alternative to shanks' mare was a bicycle, which I did not have.

Quite a few kids rode bikes to school. But the elite had mopeds. Hardly anyone could afford such an extravagance. I certainly couldn't. They were the coolest of the cool.

I wanted a bike too, but it was not merely to join their ranks. I did not want a bike to be cool or to fit in. Not exactly.

Just then the banshee wail of a two-stroke motorcycle pierced the air and I knew without having to look that it was a Yamaha. Soon enough, the bike streaked past, the rider wearing an ear to ear grin from the sheer joy of speed and sound combined in two wheels as he banked into a corner.

I stared with unadulterated envy. It was an RD350. That was a real bike! I would have given anything to be on it. As driver or pillion passenger, I didn't care. Everyone said that RD stood for *race derived*. I had no idea if that was true, but it sure looked it.

For months I had wanted a motorbike so badly that it actually hurt. That was the reason for my needing a job of course. I had to save a lot of money if I was going to get my own wheels!

I made my way to the High Street with the hope that there might be some parked motorcycles which I could gawk at.

The sun was relentless, and I was parched. I stopped and stared in through a store window at the cold drinks on display. The cans were practically dancing and calling out for me to come in and buy one. I had some loose change in my pocket thanks to having sold my lunch that day for a discounted price. I could do this since I got meal vouchers. Money was such a scarce commodity that I was willing to trade my only decent meal for a little. But easy come, easy go. I pushed open the door and was halfway inside when something made me stop.

That motorcycle was long gone, but I could still hear its high-pitched tone as it changed gears, running to its redline again and again. What must it be like to ride that bike? It angered me that I might never know.

That sound was an admonition; a reminder of what was important. I needed to save every single penny if I was ever going to get a bike. No drink for me!

I had a bank account with twenty pounds and some change. That wasn't much, at least when it came to buying a motorcycle, but I was determined to keep adding to it. And my new job was going to really make a difference. If I was diligent, I could probably save enough to buy a bike by November or December, just in time for my sixteenth birthday, when I would legally be allowed to ride it. That was still six months away. I could do it.

I turned about and continued walking. I could get a drink once I got home. Water was free.

* * *

This willingness to be frugal is a critical requirement to living outside of society (which for many, cruising is). Unless you are determined to hold down a fulltime job while sailing (and good luck with that) penny pinching has to become second nature.

This is not something that I have adhered to all my life, but when necessary I am capable of extreme focus in order to achieve my goals. Just like buying my first motorbike, when it came to funding Delphinus there was only one mechanism that I knew would work; spend nothing, sell everything and save.

When I was a kid, I had nothing to sell, so getting a job was my only option. But twenty years later, it was a very different story.

Of course, there is no getting away from spending altogether. After all, you have to eat, you need a place to live and it might be nice to have electricity and running water. There are clearly some things that one cannot do without.

But do you need cable TV? Do you need several magazine subscriptions? Do you need a gym membership for a gym that you rarely, if ever, visit?

If you are renting a big house, can you move to a smaller apartment? After all, do you really need a four bedroom, two and a half bath urban mansion?

Moving to a smaller place has other benefits than just cheaper rent, or a lower mortgage. For example, when we lived in a rather large house, we used roughly three to four thousand kilowatts of electricity, monthly. However, when we moved to a tiny apartment, our electrical consumption fell to about three to four *hundred* kilowatts. That is ten percent of the previous electrical usage.

The savings from this alone were substantial. Not to mention that everything seemed to cost less, as there were simply fewer rooms to maintain, clean, etc.

Moving to a small place might sound difficult if you have kids. But if you are planning to move aboard a boat then they will have to share their space anyway, so get them started adjusting early by sharing a room.

They, like you, should learn to make do. If you

must have a coffee when you go to work, skip Starbucks and make it yourself. Take a little extra time and save that money. Invest in a thermos flask. Not only does it save you money daily, but you can use the flask when you move aboard your boat. They come in super handy, especially on overnight passages. And if you really want to embrace the philosophy of 'stingy knows best,' buy the thermos for a quarter at a garage sale!

And while you are busy making that coffee, make yourself some lunch to go with it. If you find that you are not much of a chef, don't worry. Sandwiches are easy to make and inexpensive. Peanut butter and jelly was a childhood favorite (it still is) and you cannot get much cheaper than that. However, if that does not ring your bell, be creative and make something that you do like.

The savings on lunches at work can add up to hundreds of dollars a month. This one simple act can provide funds that, over time, make a real difference to your cruising kitty.

Once I had become serious about the whole 'living on a boat thing,' I needed to get a handle on my finances. I sat down and listed all the family outgoings. This included the mortgage, the car, insurance, travel costs, cable, phone bill, etc. Anything and everything I could think of went into a spreadsheet.

Then I estimated our monthly food bill. When I looked at the bottom line, it was clear that we could not possibly save anything unless we were willing to make drastic cuts to practically all aspects of our life.

This probably does not come as a surprise. You already know this, at least intuitively. But if you have not gone through the process described above, you should. It is a most salutary and depressing exercise, but it will immediately highlight where major savings can be made. All you need to do is make a choice.

"Do I want to have a boat and change my life? Or should I keep paying for lightning fast Internet access and cable TV?"

Cut back. Reduce EVERYTHING.

If you have an expensive car, sell it. You do not need the payments and it is only losing money as it depreciates. I know that an older car can be false economy, since they tend to go wrong more often and cost more in maintenance, but you need to learn how to maintain the vehicle yourself anyway. This is a transferable life skill which will stand you in good stead when you have to look after your boat's systems, particularly the engine. Plus, with an older car, you can reduce your insurance to liability only, which will be a huge saving.

And if you have a second car, well . . . you know what to do!

I did not need to be a financial wizard to see that it was a practical impossibility to save, so long as we kept going as we were. If that sounds like your own situation, then unless you believe that you'll win the state lottery, you must try an approach that, while painful, *will* work.

Stop spending, sell everything you own *and save.*

Your first port of call should be the big-ticket items. House, insurance, car, etc. I paid off my car and reduced insurance to liability only. That was a big saving. But it was a trade-off, since I knew that any damage to the vehicle was coming out of my pocket.

Cancel the credit cards, the cable TV, the gym, etc. Cancel everything that does not materially support your ability to live and continue to save. If you are not willing to cancel an unnecessary expense, then maybe you should question your commitment. Just how much do you want to change your life?

But life without a little luxury is not much of a life at all. So maybe treat your family to a night out once a month. *Not more.* Remember, every penny you spend means a smaller boat, an older outboard, or some other compromise. Stay strong, and save.

As strange as it may seem, what you need to be happy and healthy is a fraction of what you have. All that 'stuff' that you filled your house with is just wasted money. Stop buying and start selling.

Long after I embraced the concept of minimalism, I came across a couple of guys who were writing about it, living it, and had some very good practical ideas on how to implement minimalism in everyday life. Their names are Millburn and Nicodemus. Check them out. Nicodemus describes how he got hooked on the movement in a blog article.

"We decided to pack all my belongings as if I were moving. And then I would unpack only the items I needed over the next three weeks."

So he did exactly that. He packed everything away in boxes. When he wanted something, he would go look for it, take it out and use it. After a few weeks he had stopped looking for things. And he still had dozens of packed boxes full of the stuff that he did not really need. In a short time, he had discovered exactly what was necessary for him and what was not.

And contradiction or not, the lesson is this; what is key to our life is generally not what we actually spend our time and money on.

This is especially true when we visit the grocery store. We often spend far too much money on things we don't need, and often don't even want.

I have to guard against temptation from breads, cookies and cakes at all times. In fact, a good tip with regards to shopping is to try to avoid the supermarket when you are hungry. In my experience, that is when I make the worst choices and am the most vulnerable to spontaneous purchases.

Once you have identified the basic foodstuffs that you need to survive, create a weekly shopping list. This list is all you need, nothing more. Do not be tempted by 'two for one' offers, or special deals. If it is not on the list, ignore it.

This will have two effects. The first is that it will save you a lot of money, and the other is that you will save a lot of time.

You must learn to cut things out of your diet. In the first place, most processed foods are unhealthy, as they are loaded with salt, sugar and preservatives. All bad, in themselves. One of the worst offenders is potato chips. Do not buy them under any circumstances. Not only do they drain your wallet, but they provide zero nutritional value. Why consume a bag of grease and pay for the privilege?

The same applies to sodas, another hot topic issue area for me. Once you have started cruising, you will not need or want them, so why not eliminate them now and save the expense?

I know it can be hard to walk away from junk food, as it is designed to be addictive. This is my own Achilles heel, and I understand fully just how difficult it can be to change the eating habits of a lifetime, but change you must.

When you shop, stick to generic brands and basic foodstuffs. If you cannot get used to eating like this before you cast off, then you will not be able to live on a boat anyway. There are no freezers on budget sailboats. At least, not on mine! There are no ice machines and luxury products. What you get is compromise, hardship, and the knowledge that you only answer to yourself. Believe me, that last point is worth any amount of privation when it comes to your diet, so stick to the plan.

Save your pennies and your pounds. Then you can start the real work; selling everything you own. You could be sitting on a small fortune right now. You know that dainty little tea cup that you hate? Sell it on E-bay. And those rusty shears in the garden shed could be worth a buck or two. Have a garage sale!

Sell anything that has any value at all. Sell your radio, your sofa, your massage chair, the second car, the motorcycle and your CD or record collection. Sell your books, your clothes and your bed. The more you sell, the more you save and the closer to reality you can make your dream.

In real terms, you will need to reduce your belongings by at least 90% before you can even think of moving aboard a boat. The sooner you get used to that idea, the better.

This has two purposes. One is to liquidate assets in order to buy your boat and fund your dream. But the other is just as important. You need to declutter your life.

I have seen many people take this approach and do quite well, quickly saving enough money to get a solid boat and get sailing. But sadly, more than a few friends chose a different path. They used what they saved as a down payment, and then got a loan for the remainder to buy a boat way outside their budget.

I personally think that doing this is a big mistake. By tying yourself to a monthly payment you are merely exchanging one yoke for another. Do not fall into the trap of once again living beyond your means. In so doing, unless you really *can* work full-time while cruising, you are effectively ensuring years of continued servitude to a corporate master.

But, you might argue, if you are living on your boat,

where is the harm if you have to make monthly payments for it?

Well, if living aboard is the sum of your goals then by all means, borrow money and stay in debt. All you have done is moved to a floating condo, and no doubt you will continue to spend all you earn.

Personally, I prefer to eliminate debt entirely and enjoy a simpler and much less stressful existence. I will admit that this means doing without many things, but I would argue that the benefits of a minimalist lifestyle far outweigh the negatives.

So, do yourself a favor. If you have only twenty thousand dollars, then look for a boat that costs no more than fifteen thousand. Or, even better, ten thousand bucks. You might be scraping the bottom of the barrel, but you would be surprised what even that can get you.

In fact, there are those who have successfully obtained a boat (usually in very rough shape) for free, and then used sweat equity and minimal cash to bring it back to usable condition, all while living aboard and saving on rent.

Many boat yards and marinas have a corner where the more or less abandoned boats stand, so maybe that is an option? Keep an eye out. Even if a boat does not have a for sale sign on it, that does not mean that the owner would not offload it gladly.

If I could offer one key piece of advice it would be this; be ready to adjust your expectations. It is far better to go simple and go now than to have the best possible boat years down the line.

Nothing drives me nuts more than people saying that this boat or that boat was good, but the dinette was the wrong layout, or they did not like the countertops in the galley. Such frippery is foolish. When you are crossing the Gulf Stream for the first time, I am sure you will not be thinking that you wished it was in a boat with Corian countertops. And when you drop anchor off a small Greek island, I am sure you will not hide yourself in shame, fearing that some other cruiser will see your dinette and feel bad for you.

If you want to change your life, maybe you first need to change yourself. This is no easy task. Getting rid of the trappings of our materialist society is not just about making some money to put towards your boat, it is about changing your attitude and *becoming a different person.*

To live on a boat, you must first adopt a minimalist lifestyle *and love it.* Trust me, none of the things that you currently own will be useful to you in the future if you want to go cruising. Of course, there are some exceptions. The camera, the laptop, yes they are good and some might even say necessary in this day and age. But your prom dress? Nope. Twenty pairs of shoes? I don't think so. A huge library of books? Not a chance.

The list of things that you do not need is infinitely longer than the list of things that you *do.*

If you can make a penny from anything, sell it. Don't even think twice. Whatever pain you feel from selling something is nothing compared to the pain you will feel when you have to give it away, or worse, throw it away, because the time has come to finally make the move.

Plus, and I cannot stress this enough, in a very short time you will not miss any of it. Once your accumulated clutter is all gone, you will feel a great weight lift from your shoulders. Let the stuff go and be free. It is an amazing experience and you will wonder why you did not do it long ago.

So, forget about paying for storage or using your

parent's basement to stash your LPs. Just get rid of all the junk. The more brutal you can be with yourself, the better off you will be, financially, emotionally and perhaps most importantly, spiritually.

Without wishing to get too Zen here, I want to make a very important point. Material objects weigh us down. They choke us and drown us.

Do you remember the scene from the movie Labyrinth, where the junk lady gives Jennifer Connelly her teddy bear, Sir Lancelot? And then proceeds to load her up with all the memories of her childhood, piling them onto her back like a defensive shell? Just like the junk lady, your possessions will keep you rooted in one place, and eventually they will entomb you. As painful as it may seem, you have to cast them away.

Remember, all you need is your boat. And it will set you free.

Chapter 6 – The moral dilemma

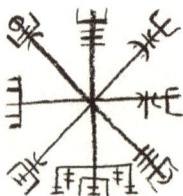

"Do not let your fire go out."

~ Ayn Rand

I have struggled for a very long time with a dilemma. Namely, how do I want to live my life? In fact, for more than thirty years, I have yearned to make a fundamental change in what I do, how I live and who I am. That is not because my life has not been good, because it has. By any objective standard of measuring such things, you would say that I have done 'okay' if not been downright blessed.

But at the risk of sounding very selfish, that is not enough and I want more. Or at least, and I think this is the important point, I want something *different*.

Like most people, I have a job which takes up most of my time. I go to work early and I come home tired, then I get a couple of hours to be with my wife and kids before I need to hit the sack. The next day, I repeat the cycle.

Why do I do this? Is it to buy a bigger house? A newer car? Frankly, I am not very interested in these things. I like them but they do not define me and they do not make me happy, especially when I know how much they cost. I would like to say that material trappings are mostly meaningless to me, and yet I find myself consistently acquiring new things.

I am a contemplative sort of fellow, and I have given some thought to why I do this. One does not need to be a therapist to define my problem. For the last thirty years, I have been making choices that were best for my family and *rarely* for me.

It is important for me to note that this was my choice. I chose to be a husband and a father, and it is a sacred duty that I take seriously. And while I would love the freedom to follow my bliss, I would not do it at any cost.

Now, I would not say that I have been unhappy for the better part of my adult life, but I have been restless and to some degree dissatisfied. I find myself constantly looking to the horizon, or examining boats and even vans with a critical eye, gauging their ability to carry me far, far away.

That wanderlust I had in my teens as I explored the English countryside on my motorcycle has never gone, and it continues to worry at me like a dog with a bone.

As a result, I tried to assuage my discontent with shiny toys; a nice guitar, a motorbike, a new car. These were pointless, wasteful distractions that amused and entertained for a short time, but ultimately left a sour taste in both my mouth and my soul.

Make no mistake, I am not ungrateful for what I have. But I do not value it above the experience that living a life free of the nine to five grind demands.

Could I leave my family to pursue my dream? No. The thought does not even cross my mind. I firmly believe that a man owes it to his family to take care of and provide for them. As I said, it is a sacred duty and I will always do my best. My oldest kids are both adults now, and they are good people, so I think I probably did an okay job.

But I have played the role of husband, father and breadwinner to the best of my ability for almost thirty years. And that is where my dilemma lies. I am now coming into the last third of my life and I have not achieved my most cherished of personal ambitions. And though it goes against the grain, I am beginning to think that the ethical egoists have a point; perhaps it is time for me to starting demanding what *I need* and worry less about what other people want.

Is this a midlife crisis? Some might think so, although I do not. I like to think of it more as a midlife awakening. And what evidence do I have to support my hypothesis? Well, for one I have no urge to get a sports car! But I do question my life choices and the goals that have been defined for me.

When I think about the future, I remember Dan from South Bend and I am confirmed in my desire to make a change. After all, do I really want to go dutifully to work every day, hating every minute of it, just so that I can finally retire and start to live? That was Dan's plan and look where it got him. Frankly, I am not willing to wait or take the chance that I won't even make it to retirement.

Yet I cannot just throw caution to the wind as I have responsibilities to my family. And unless I suddenly win the lottery, it is impossible for me to be everything, to everyone.

And therein lies the rub. How do I balance the demands of society, family and conscience against my own needs, and somehow still make it work?

I suspect that there is no single answer to that question. What works for me, might not work for you and vice versa.

After all, when it comes to the practical aspects of giving up your current life, moving aboard a boat and learning to live a life with deliberate meaning, then there is no wrong or right way to go about it. Simply put, whatever floats your boat (a silly pun, I know, but I could not resist) is the solution.

Still, perhaps my (many) failings can serve as a cautionary tale? Having read this book, you will hopefully learn certain things that you could avoid, and perhaps glean some ideas on what you *can* do to make your dream a reality. Of course, it does not matter if you follow my approach or anything that I advise. After all, we do not need to agree with everyone all of the time, right?

But agreement can be important, especially if you are trying to persuade your significant other to adopt your dream and follow you.

Just as an example, I knew a pair of lovebirds who wrangled over the type of boat that would be suitable for their long-term needs as a cruising couple. While this may sound like an entirely reasonable discussion to have, it was not. One party demanded what was essentially a luxury yacht, while the other would have been perfectly happy with a well-used, twenty-year-old production sailboat.

Their needs were polar opposites and ultimately irreconcilable. Basic but functional, versus high end luxury. There must always be a middle ground.

Clearly, someone has to adjust their expectations. And so long as both partners are willing to compromise, then I believe a future together is possible. But when an individual is unyielding, then only one outcome is likely. And that is why you can often find a bargain boat for sale.

This disparity between what one partner wants, and what the other considers necessary is a relatively common problem that I have seen amongst cruising couples and one that I faced myself on many occasions while both living aboard and as a regular Joe Schmo with a house and job.

Of course, everything is a tradeoff. Life is nothing if not a series of endless negotiations and compromises. You cannot always know what the best course of action is going to be. Sometimes you have to just roll the dice and hope for the best.

One question that almost everyone who wants to live life on the water asks is, should they go now with very little, or maybe go later with much more?

I inserted the maybe into that question because the future is uncertain. You can never know what may happen. Will you and your partner still be together in ten years? Will you still have your health in five?

I felt that the way I was going with my stress ridden lifestyle there was a good chance that I would be on the wrong side of both of those questions.

So, my advice to you is to go now, with whatever you have. Believe it or not, you don't really need all that much. Most likely, you CAN do it right now. You just need to be willing to make sacrifices and adjust your expectations. It does not matter if you have to assume some risks. There are risks associated to any decision we make. But I would rather make the wrong choice than not get to choose at all.

And that was my philosophy when I started on the road to the sea. I could have worked longer, saved more and bought a bigger boat. But I was not willing to wait. I wanted to feel the salt spray on my face, and I was literally willing to jump in with both feet.

But first, I just had to sell everything I owned.

Chapter 7 – Watch the Baby

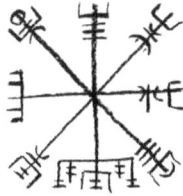

"The proper function of man is to live, not to exist. I shall not waste my days in trying to prolong them. I shall use my time."

~ *Jack London*

Once Kate and I had made the decision to buy a boat, I went into hardcore planning mode. We were starting with a negative bank balance and considerable debt, including credit cards, car and house payments.

I knew that we would have to eliminate practically everything that we had accrued in the last couple of years and that it would not be easy to let some of it go.

Thus began the period of great debates, as we critically examined everything from the perspective of living aboard a sailboat.

"Should we keep this?" Kate asked, lifting up a large hardback coffee table book on renaissance art. We both loved it but it did not fit the very narrow criteria of 'boat stuff.'

"Nope," I replied. "It's too big, too heavy."

"But it was expensive!"

"Yeah, I know. But we can't keep it."

"But . . ."

"Sorry. We have to sell it."

"Okay," Kate rather reluctantly conceded. "What

about this one?" She held up a book about the Beatles, my all-time favorite group. I really loved that book, a photographic journey of the Fab Four during their all too short career. I would have to be strong. Sigh.

"Put it on the pile."

And so it went. In the end, the 'for sale' pile was more than 90% of everything we owned.

A simple test, for those who feel that the above scenario is unimaginably hard is to ask yourself a question regarding any object in your home. "Have you used it in the last six months?"

If the answer is "No" then you do not really need it, whatever it is.

We used the last of our time in Chicago to sell, give away and generally dispose of anything that would not fit into our Ford Explorer and that we knew was not essential to our future lifestyle. That single sentence makes it sound easy, but the truth is that it was a long and painful process. I loved a good many of the things we got rid of. But we were on a mission. A higher power was calling us to a new life, and sacrifices had to be made!

Eventually, we got down to the bare basics, with clothes, tools, a guitar, baby things, some sailing books and other bits and pieces we thought we could not live without. A few precious things, like some antique books we could not part with, were packed off to Kate's family in Norway, where they would reside for the foreseeable future. All we had to do now was pack the car and set off.

I had spent a lot of time looking on the Internet, and there were many hundreds of boats that we could afford available in the US. Finding and buying one would be easy, I reasoned. Finding a place where we could dock it would be a little harder, but I was full of optimism. After all, there are thousands of marinas too. Or so I thought.

The reason that I had not already done my research on liveaboard marinas was due to the fact that we still had not decided on *where* we were going. All I knew was that I wanted to live on the coast. Which coast had not been decided, and in truth did not really matter to me.

I had joined many online forums researching potential locations for our future floating home, and eventually I came to an approximate decision; the West Coast, and either San Diego or San Francisco, or the East Coast, and anywhere from Baltimore down to Raleigh. West or East? Both options appeared to offer a great deal, and I would have been happy with either, but I could not decide as they seemed equal in my eyes.

Of course, as this was the United States, I thought that maybe I should follow Greeley's advice and go west. Perhaps that was *my* manifest destiny?

Besides, San Diego sounded good. It was likely to be always sunny, unlike San Francisco, but either city would be a fine choice. After several winters in Chicago, California had a strong appeal. But Baltimore or Annapolis offered distinct seasons, which is also a very attractive feature. Nothing beats east coast Fall colors for beauty.

I did not know much about any of the cities, except what I had seen on television. San Francisco had a bridge and was very hilly, which apparently resulted in motor vehicles spending an inordinate amount of time airborne, while San Diego had a zoo and was close to Mexico. This was not much to base a major life decision on.

One place, in particular, was a mystery; Annapolis. Years previously, I had read Alex Hailey's book, Roots, from which I learned that his forefather was sold in

Annapolis as a slave. Not a fact, it must be said, conducive to persuading me to live there.

But as the time to leave grew closer, we had to make a decision. It was not so much that I could not decide, simply that I did not really have a preference, one way or the other.

I looked to Kate, and then at the road atlas lying on the coffee table. That table was practically the only piece of furniture left. The new owner of our apartment had expressed an interest in it, so we were leaving it as a sort of house-warming present.

"Shall we use the Magic Eight Ball?" I asked.

"Can't," she replied. "I gave it away."

"What? Who to?"

"I don't know his name. One of the neighbor's kids."

I had received the Eight Ball as a leaving present from my colleagues just a few days before, so I was irked that Kate had given it away. Then it struck me that I really had no use for it. It was just more clutter. I was glad that someone would enjoy it. Immediately I felt fine about her decision.

"Never mind. We have something better."

I fished around in my pocket and produced my lucky quarter. It was struck in 1941, which meant that the coin was about 90% silver. I got it in my change one day from a deli and I had since hung onto it as a good luck charm.

For anyone interested in numismatics, I can tell you that it was minted in San Francisco, as it had an 'S' stamp, but its value to a collector was negligible due to wear.

One can always rely on this most ancient of decision making systems. The Romans referred to it as 'navia aut caput,' or ship and head, while in medieval England tossing a coin was called 'cross and pile,' thanks to the markings found on the face and back of the coins at that time.

Clearly, the practice of making an important decision with a coin toss goes far beyond merely the kick-off in a game of football. In fact, in 1845, the city of Portland was so named after a coin toss. The alternative under consideration was Boston. I guess it could have been worse.

A little later, in 1903, one of mankind's greatest achievements was decided by the flip of a coin when the Wright brothers decided who would attempt the first manned flight. Wilbur won, giving him the right. His attempt was not very successful however, so Orville got all the glory with the *second* flight. A good example of when losing the toss is advantageous!

I did not think my own coin toss was quite as momentous as the above examples, but it's nice to be in such august company.

I placed the coin on the tips of my fingers.

"Heads for the west coast, tails for the east," I said and tossed the coin into the air, where it span around and around before falling and ringing to a stop on the floor. We bent closer to look. Tails.

"Great! Good decision," I declared. After all, if you're in the market for a sailboat, the east coast, and Annapolis is one of the best locations in the world. From there, you have access to boats all along the eastern side of the US, assuming that you cannot find anything to take your fancy in the Chesapeake Bay.

"So, we leave tomorrow then?" Kate asked.

We both looked around the apartment. It was bare. Just some wires where the TV has been, the coffee table, an empty pizza box and the ghostly outline on the walls where some pictures had once hung. Everything we now owned was in our bedroom, stacked, bagged and boxed.

"I guess we should start loading the car," I replied with a nod.

As it happened, we set off two days later after handing over the keys a little early to the apartment's new owner. Our real estate broker did not mind organizing things ahead of schedule and everything went smoothly. The money from the sale was on its way to our account and we were heading east.

It was early in the morning in late January, and we made the 720-mile drive to Maryland in two very long days. This might seem a little slow, but with a baby in the car and Kate pregnant (yes, baby number two was on the way) one has to stop more frequently than one might wish. Bathroom breaks were essential for both mother and child.

A Howard Johnson put us up the first night we were on the road, and in the evening of the second day, we arrived in Annapolis.

The city was settled in the mid-17th century, and is situated on the mouth of the Severn River. This little tidbit is something of an odd coincidence for me, since I had known the Severn well for a good many years, but in the United Kingdom! In fact, I had grown up just a few short miles from the second fastest tidal river in the world. With an average tide of 48 feet, or 15 meters, it is a treacherous stretch of water and has claimed many lives. Hopefully this new Severn River would be a bit tamer, especially since we might well be sailing on it.

Having arrived in town, we ran into our first problem. I had assumed that it would be easy to find short term lodgings in the city itself, but there were several conferences being hosted that week in or around Annapolis, and there was simply no room at the inn. Actually, there were plenty of hotels, but they were exceedingly expensive. Also, some of them refused to accept families with children. Or dogs. Okay, we did not have a dog, but I took issue with the fact that our daughter was considered to be on a par with someone else's pooch.

I made a lot of phone calls trying to locate an affordable place to establish our base of operations, getting further and further out of town until finally I found a motel we could afford. It was not ideal, but it would do. The only problem was that we could only have it for a week, since there were bookings for yet another conference.

Now that we had a toe hold in Annapolis, I was sure we could find another motel before we were kicked out. So we set up camp and got to straight to work. The first thing we did was meet up with a friendly yacht broker. I think we did well when we met with Fran. She took a shine to us, particularly to Kate and our daughter, and she went out of her way to be helpful.

We made an appointment the next day to see some boats with her and we drove to the marina where she had an office. It just so happened that there were a number of boats in the yard that might meet our needs. These were boats that had seen better days, but that was fine with us. We had a limited budget, and we knew we would have to start on the bottom rung of the boating ladder. Fran took us to have a look at the first on the list of 'possibles.'

I was excited to be finally getting my hands dirty, both figuratively and literally and I set to examining the first boat with gusto.

"What do you think?" Fran asked, raising one eyebrow interrogatively, her demeanor carefully neutral.

Fran was a tiny woman, with a wizened face and ready smile. Her energy and humor were infectious, and we were buoyed up with excitement.

Until we saw the first boat on her list.

The Hunter 27 had been on the hard for a while. It was old, tired and worn out, so I felt an instant affinity with it. On the plus side, it was quite roomy. Thanks to its wide beam and layout, I thought that it would make a good budget liveaboard. However, I had a set of criteria in mind and it didn't tick all the boxes. We did not just want a floating home, we wanted something that could sail offshore, and with a moderate degree of safety. I was serious about our mission and unwilling to compromise.

I had read what I could on self-assessing a sailboat. I am no surveyor, but some things are pretty obvious and after thirty minutes of kicking the tires I had formed an opinion.

"The foresail is ripped, it has no running rigging, there are no anchors or chain and one of the main winches is seized. And it smells of mold. I'm guessing the seller is very motivated."

Fran smiled. It was not an unfair assessment. After two years being stored under an oak tree, the boat was becoming a liability, both to its owner and the yard. Every month that passed, a little more of its value drained away as more leaves and debris piled up on its already filthy deck. In another year or two, it would probably be next to worthless.

"True, but it's really cheap," she said with an urchin grin and twinkle in her eye.

It *was* cheap, I could not argue with that. A boat that we could easily afford. 'Cheap' had been one of the conditions I had given Fran. I also dictated that it should be a good coastal cruiser, if not Blue Water capable. Instead of showing us the door, she had shown us the Hunter. But it would require spending more on a refit than the boat itself was worth. Much more, in fact.

"Let's look at the next on the list," I said.

She nodded, and led us to the next candidate, a Pearson 30. This one looked far more promising. In the first place, it was actually in the water. It also had a furling genoa and running rigging, and there was even an anchor at the bow.

All in all, it was a sweet looking vessel, albeit somewhat narrow.

"This is at the top of your budget," Fran said. "Oh, and it has an Atomic 4."

I frowned. All the forums I had frequented had warned about those. The Universal Atomic 4 was a gas-powered engine designed to run in the marine environment. People either loved or hated them. The fact that many people replaced them with a diesel engine spoke volumes to me.

Still, there was a hardcore group of sailors who maintained that they were perfectly fine engines, so long as they were cared for. I would try keep an open mind.

I climbed aboard first, then Kate passed our daughter over the lifelines. I placed her down in the cockpit and held her hand until Fran, then Kate had climbed aboard. Then I gave Kate 'the nod.' As was our habit, we passed responsibility for keeping an eye on our little girl back and forth. This was generally an unspoken negotiation, made with eye contact, nods, and expressions. We did not need a verbal agreement to know who was currently responsible for her.

Having just passed Kate the 'baton,' so to speak, I moved towards the mast, keen to examine the gooseneck. Kate firmly parked our daughter on the raised coamings around the cockpit, where our little angel gurgled happily. Then she leaned back against the For-Sale sign attached to the lifelines. Who would have thought that she could slip through? We certainly didn't. It was only when we heard a splash that we understood. Our daughter had fallen overboard.

I spun around to see both Kate and Fran leaning over the side of the boat with looks of horror on their faces. I intuited at once what had happened, and without a second thought I leaped over the lifelines, crashing down into the dark, frigid water with a huge splash. I had just enough time to see that our daughter was floating on her back, buoyed up by the many layers of her thick clothing. And like a monster rising from the depths, I came up from below her, kicking as hard as I could. I grasped our baby in both hands and raised her into the air, whereupon Kate snatched her back to safety. Then, my momentum spent, I went under again my mind flashing back to a similar incident some years previously.

Interlude, May 1991

I surfaced from under the brown, slow moving water, desperately keeping my mouth firmly closed and a steady stream of air bubbling from my nose. The Nile is not the cleanest of rivers, and it is entirely possible to get sick as a result of swimming in it. In fact, one in twelve of Egypt's citizens suffer from schistosomiasis, otherwise known as bilharzia, a rather nasty urinary tract and intestinal disease caused by parasitic flatworms. I had no desire to be one of them.

A young American woman named Agnes helped pull me back aboard onto the low deck of the felucca. I had been knocked off by a rather angry goat, much to the glee of the lateen sailed vessel's captain who grinned at me toothlessly.

Spluttering and coughing I glared my indignation

at the animal but in moments I was laughing too. It was only my pride that was hurt, as the creature had butted me in the behind, sending me overboard with a great splash.

I sat on the deck and the young woman's boyfriend passed me a water bottle. I used some to rinse my mouth and then my eyes. I was not entirely sure just how those parasites entered the body, but I did not want to take a chance. There was nothing much I could do with being wet though as I did not have more than a spare T-shirt to change into. But that hardly mattered. I was dry again in just a few minutes thanks to the mid-day heat.

We had all signed on for a three-day cruise along the river Nile onboard a traditional Egyptian boat. It had only a single great sail which was raised on a long pole. Unlike similar gaff rigged sailboats, where the roughly square sail is raised by hoisting a spar or pole attached to the sail's head, the felucca has a triangular sail, the longest edge of which is tied to an exceedingly spindly looking wooden spar.

I was travelling alone, having recently parted with my current girlfriend. We had met on the *so called* express train to Luxor, a twenty-four-hour journey comprising extreme heat and discomfort. Perhaps it was just the shared adversity of the train ride that brought us together, but we hit it off and became inseparable. At least, I thought we were, but I was to later discover that we had some fundamental differences. Yet we traveled together, growing close as we journeyed through Egypt and Israel, then Jordan and Palestine.

After travelling together for three months, we finally parted ways in Siwa, an oasis far to the east of Alexandria and once home to the oracle of Ammon. According to Arrian of Nicomedia, Alexander the

Great had gone there to ask if he was the son of Ammon. That is to say, the son of God.

When I went there I had no questions for the oracle, as it had long fallen into ruin. But I did have some questions for my girlfriend when she dumped me.

I was heartbroken at her choice to return to Germany but I was not ready to go home myself. I chose to continue my travels in the ancient land of Egypt and experience everything it had to offer. That was when I decided to take a tour on the water with a group of strangers.

The days were long on the boat, exposed as we were to the relentless sun. There was no cover. No cabins, and only a shallow hold that was little more than a bilge. We slept on deck and spent our days talking, sleeping, playing my guitar and singing out of key, and of course enjoying the scenery that slipped past at barely walking speed.

Once in a while a large cruise ship would churn past, throwing out a heavy wake that caused our boat to buck and dive. But we never looked at the tourists enjoying their ice-cold beverages and shaded deck chairs with envy.

We were at peace with the heat and the flies and the lack of facilities as we gained something that the hoi polloi on their expensive cruise ships did not; a genuine connection with the boat's crew and their country.

The half dozen passengers on the felucca were from various lands, and communication was mostly done in English, with French and German making an occasional appearance. Our hosts spoke Arabic, and very limited English, but we made do with sign language and much waving of hands.

With each day we felt more like a part of the crew,

as we helped to steer, or raise the sail, or cook the day's meal. This last task ultimately included the goat that assaulted my buttocks, so I guess I got my revenge, and very tasty it was too.

At night, we lay awake watching the stars wheel across the sky as we hunkered down in our sleeping bags. For such a hot country, it sure could get cold at night. But I did not mind. I was used to being cold, a trait that has frequently come in handy.

* * *

Kate and Fran immediately rushed away (into a nearby office, as I was later to discover) while I was left to my own devices splashing around between the boats. I am a big, heavy man, so there was no way that I could climb back aboard on my own. Especially as there was no swim ladder. No, I would have to make my way out between the docks and hope for a ladder attached to a piling. I found one, thirty yards away.

Since it was January, the water was bitterly cold and I was really starting to feel it by the time I clambered out. But worse was to come. Once out of the water, the wind chill had an immediate effect, and I hurried to the yacht brokerage's office, barely able to operate the door handle with my now stiff fingers. Inside the office it was wonderfully warm and I found Kate and Fran dressing our little mermaid in a fresh outfit on one of the sofas.

I was keen to get out of my own wet clothes, unfortunately I had not planned for this eventuality and there was nothing I could change into. All our belongings were stashed in the motel. And unlike my accidental dip in the Nile, I would not dry out quite so quickly in Maryland in mid-winter.

Of course, our daughter was fine since she had a

complete spare set of clothing available, and incredibly, the water had not actually had time to soak through everything, but I had to spend several uncomfortable hours very slowly drying out.

In spite of our potentially deadly mishap, we had a schedule and felt keenly the need to stick to it. Instead of going back to the motel and calling it a day we pressed on.

That was an inauspicious start to our boating life and perhaps should have served as a warning of things to come. But once I had recouped a modicum of body heat, Fran took us to another marina, and then another. We looked at many boats and she gave us a lot of useful information about their histories and construction methods and general seaworthiness.

Fran was a kind soul who took a pair of wannabes under her wing and tried to guide us into making an informed decision. But working within our limited budget wasn't easy.

We made a concerted effort to examine every boat in the Annapolis area that was even remotely close to what we could afford. However, nothing 'rang my bell' and I told Fran that I would call her in a day or two after I had reviewed my notes.

In the meantime, I went further and further afield, checking out any listings that looked likely. When nothing in Maryland met my criteria, I bundled Kate and our daughter into the car and took them on excursions to Delaware or Virginia. I would drive for hours and hours on the off chance that a listing was as good or better than it sounded. This was rarely the case and I began to despair that we would be able to afford anything at all. Had we made a huge mistake in coming to Annapolis? We were spending more than I liked (eating out every day is not cheap) and there was another problem about to rear its head.

Chapter 8 – A Lucky Find

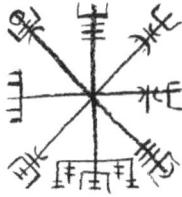

"The best luck of all is the luck you make for yourself."
~ Douglas MacArthur

"Hey, Mr. Kobernus. I'm sorry, but I'm gonna need you folks out by eleven tomorrow."

The portly motel manager seemed genuinely apologetic as he waved to me from across the car park. I closed the car door carefully, so as not to wake my daughter who was fast asleep in the back and made my way over to him. As much as it made problems for us, I understood. We had taken the room knowing we had only a week so this was not a surprise.

"Yeah, sure. No worries. Any chance another motel around here has a vacancy?" I asked, knowing already what the answer would be.

He grimaced and shook his head. "Doubt it. The conference organizers block book hundreds of rooms at a time. I'd bet my bottom dollar most of the motels are tied up right now."

This too was not news to me as I had already tried to find another motel with zero result. In spite of my best efforts we could not find an affordable (read cheap) alternative anywhere in the vicinity. There were plenty of hotels and B&Bs and such, but their rates were simply more than we could justify.

But luck was with us that day, even if we were about to become homeless. While at the library, checking online 'boat for sale' websites I found a listing for a sailboat that I had never heard of before; a Seafarer. It was not very far from Annapolis, as the boat was located in a marina in Deale. I called the listing broker and made arrangements to view it as soon as possible. We drove down later that day.

The broker met us at the marina and showed us to the boat. When I saw it, I knew instantly. This was the one. It was love at first sight!

With its fin keel, full skeg-rudder and Aries self-steering, plus a good selection of sails in reasonable shape, this looked like our best bet so far.

Incidentally, the word 'skeg' comes from the old Norwegian word for beard; 'skegg.' It is pronounced in modern Norwegian as 'sheg' and you can easily see how it relates to the English word 'shaggy.' I learned that years later, when I . . . No. You will just have to wait to hear about that part of my life.

But back to the boat! It needed a good cleaning on deck and the bottom needed to be scraped and have anti-fouling applied, but that is all part of owning a boat. Plus the batteries were toast and the electronics were ancient (it even had a loran for goodness sake) but that was not unexpected. At least it had a recent VHF radio.

According to the specs, the boat weighed in at 10,300 lbs, with 4,850 of that being ballast. With her 9-foot 9-inch beam, this gave her a capsize ration of around 1.7, which is pretty good. Of course, capsize ratios can all be taken with a pinch of salt, as they do not adequately consider all variables. However, if two boats share a similar design, and one has a lower capsize ratio, you can bet that it is more stable in rough weather.

The interior of the Seafarer was very efficiently designed and looked like it would provide a safe and functional environment for offshore conditions. An adult could easily move about freely and yet have handholds and surfaces to brace against within easy reach regardless of the point of heel.

When entering the salon my eye was immediately drawn to the chart table. It was a thing of beauty and its like will not be found on many boats. It could easily accommodate a full-sized Admiralty chart on its surface without folding and still have room to spare. It was constructed from solid teak and mahogany as was the rest of the interior.

I will not pretend otherwise. I fell deeply and madly in love with that boat.

This might be the worst thing that can happen when you are considering buying anything, be it a boat, car, house, or whatever. Obviously, if you allow your heart to rule over your head then you run the risk of making a serious mistake that you will later regret.

Of course, that is why you need a professional to rein you in. I had previously contacted a marine surveyor, who promised a survey as soon as I was ready to pull the trigger on a boat, so I gave him a call and asked him to set aside time for the survey. Then I contacted Fran and gave her the details of the boat.

The survey was expensive, but well worth it. Plus, I had to pay extra as I wanted the report in record time (next day). Now, a survey is a great thing to get. Aside from the fact that you need one for insurance purposes, it also provides some easy points of negotiation, which can help reduce the asking price. In addition, it gives the buyer an instant 'to do' list for upgrades, maintenance or repairs that are necessary. It would be fair to say that the survey paid for itself, several times over.

The survey revealed that the rigging was oversized and in good condition, but there were missing split-pins in the turnbuckles. The deck was in good condition, and there were no apparent leaks.

The running rigging was not installed and appeared to be barely serviceable and he recommended replacing all the lines.

I am sure that there were other issues. Batteries, of course, to name but one, however, overall the Seafarer was revealed to be a well-found vessel with only minor problems and cosmetic issues. No delamination in the hull, no soggy deck, no seized winches.

We decided to forego a sea trial and with the survey concluded I made an offer for somewhat less than the asking price. It was accepted. In less than 24 hours, we owned the boat. Delphinus was ours!

Finally, after all those months of wishing and wanting and working towards our goal, we were nearly there. We wasted no time, and immediately got to work prepping her for her return to the water. We planned to sail Delphinus back to Annapolis and install her in a marina as soon as possible. After all, we had nowhere else to live. That boat was now our home.

We checked out of the motel and although Delphinus was still propped up on the hard, we moved aboard. Technically, the yard did not approve but we did it anyway and no one said anything. It was that or sleep in the car, and while I have certainly slept in worse places it seemed a bit of an imposition for the whole family.

But that first night aboard was not exactly ideal. The electrical systems were all offline, so there was no light. We had only some bottled water and a couple of packets of McVities' Hobnobs for dinner, but that was okay. To us, ensconced now in our new home, it was a feast. We could put up with a lot knowing that we had finally achieved our most important objective.

We had already visited all the local marinas during our boat viewing expeditions with Fran and we knew where we wanted to base ourselves as we started our new life. The marina we selected offered many essential amenities and, critically, was liveaboard friendly. Plus, we already knew one of our new neighbors, since that was where Fran's office was located.

I had already arranged for a dock space big enough to accommodate our new pride and joy. All we had to do was get her there in one piece. No small challenge for someone who has never sailed before.

But before that, as all new boat owners must, we had to go through many initiation tests, the first being the ritual scraping, sanding and painting of the hull.

Drudgery, thy name is sailing.

How our arms hurt! I hired a sander with attached vacuum from the marina and we went to work with a passion, removing old paint and smoothing the hull's seemingly vast surface. But with a gallon of blue antifouling applied the once flaky surface looked good. In fact, it looked great. The only moment of uncertainty came when we had to move the jack stands, in order to prep and paint behind them. Luckily, that too went smoothly.

We installed new zinc anodes on the prop shaft and polished the three bladed bronze propeller until it shone like the helm of a Spartan warrior. I installed brand new type 27 deep-cycle marine batteries. Have you ever carried one of those on your shoulder while climbing up a ladder? These batteries are immensely heavy (circa 75lbs, each) and they left my shoulder bruised for weeks. I did not care however, since we were making our dream real. A little bruising was a small price to pay.

It took us two days to finish prepping the boat, then we informed the yard we were ready to put her in the water. Luckily for us, someone had not finished their own annual bottom painting ritual and they were forced to reschedule their launch. The yard manager knew that we were ready to go and he kindly gave us the newly available launch slot. The next day we evacuated the boat and watched in trepidation as a very large machine came and hoisted her into the air.

We suffered ten minutes of nail-biting tension as Delphinus inched towards the dock, swinging gently in the cradle, but her launch went without a hitch.

Once in the water, however, we were at something of a loss. We could start the engine, we could steer the boat and 'in principle' we knew how to navigate. But neither of us knew how to get to Annapolis, never mind find the marina. In spite of these obvious, and somewhat serious shortcomings, I was willing to try.

"Why don't we just give it a go?" I asked, knowing full well what Kate's answer would be.

"No. We don't know the waters. Who knows what could happen."

We had paper charts, but no GPS, so being precise about our location would have been difficult. There were shoals, rocks, and who knows what else to consider. I thought for a moment.

"Okay, why don't we ask someone to help us out, someone that knows the water?"

"That's fine. But we have a baby onboard. It has to be a proper licensed captain."

I did not think it needed to be a professional licensed captain. After all, any skipper who has managed to get their boat in and out of a slip without mishap had better credentials than we did. A licensed captain seemed like overkill to me. But the look on

Kate's face left little room for discussion on this point.

"We could ask Chuck," I said, with a nod to the other side of the marina.

Thankfully, in our short time in Deale, we had acquired a contact. Having recently met some cruising folk during dinner in a nearby restaurant, I knew where professional help could be found. So long as he was willing, that is.

The O'Dells owned a sailboat temporarily docked on the side of the marina reserved for the big boats, the 50 footers, which were like palaces compared to Delphinus. Chuck O'Dell was a certified captain and had performed many boat deliveries. Surely he would love to pilot a couple of noobs and their boat to Annapolis?

I paid them a visit, and asked if he would lend a hand. Being an affable sort, he was happy to help. We struck a deal, and I hired him to deliver our boat. This was only a distance of around 20 miles by car. Of course, by boat it's a little further, what with all the twisty bits of coast, so we figured about five hours travel time and agreed a rate.

Since the running rigging was not installed and we could not raise sail, we motored the entire way. I don't think anyone minded the extra noise from the little engine. We just wanted to get our boat 'home' so that we could get settled in.

Despite the fact that it was a gray day, we were filled with excitement and good cheer as we made our way out of the marina and into Tracy's Creek. We passed Drum Point, and soon entered the Chesapeake proper. It was our first time being out on the water in our own boat and I was thrilled.

We did not quite hug the coast, but it was always visible off the port side. As we motored, I studied our chart of the bay, noting the landmarks as we passed them; Deale Beach, Columbia Beach, Snug Harbor.

We got a little excited when we chugged past the Thomas Point lighthouse. It is a beautiful structure, though it marks a dangerous shoal. Built in 1875, it looks very much like a real house, except it stands on spindly steel piles embedded in the rock. People used to live there once, operating the light, but since 1986 it has been automated. Now it is empty most of the time, but whenever I passed it I would think how it would make a great B&B. What a view it has!

Eventually we entered the channel to Back Creek, motoring past row after row of sailboats, motorboats, and luxury yachts. Minutes later we sighted the marina and friendly faces waved us into our new dock. Chuck provided instruction as I steered us towards our slip. Perhaps his confidence was contagious as I calmly turned the wheel this way and that, according to his hand gestures.

We glided in between the pilings, and before we knew it we were in our slip. Chuck helped us tie up, showing us how to correctly tie a line around a cleat, then he shook our hands and said goodbye. He had a local friend waiting to drive him back to Deale. But before he left he gave us one last piece of advice.

"Just remember," he said. "Take it easy, take it slow. You don't need to learn everything on day one."

And with that, he took his leave. I looked at Kate and our daughter and grinned. We were home. We had survived our first journey without incident. There was not even a hint of running aground or sinking from a failed seacock or improperly serviced stuffing box. Naturally, we were relieved. Especially since we still had a packet of half eaten hob-nobs to get through.

Chapter 9 – Finding our Feet

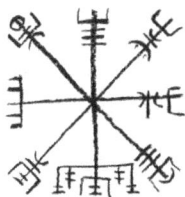

"The cure for anything is salt water
— sweat, tears, or the sea."

~ *Karen Blixen*

Since Delphinus was only 31 feet, or 9.5 meters in length, we were placed on Dock A. This was the backwater of the marina as it was extremely shallow there. It was also where a sailing school operated, so there was often something interesting to watch as students panicked trying to get the training boats in or out of the slips. Of course, we were not much different. It was like a Marx brothers' episode as we negotiated the perils of our own slip, especially as our tiny helper was desperate to get in the way.

But I thought that everything about our new home was wonderful. Even the wind keeping us awake at night as it plucked nearby halyards was good. That symphony of clangs was music to my ears, compared to the cacophonous noise of the city. Plus there was the salt smell of the water, and the camaraderie of the community and, and, and.

In fact, there was always something happening in the area. If it was not Nature itself catching our eye with the occasional Northern Water snake swimming past our slip or a horseshoe crab (which I was convinced was a rare prehistoric creature) turning up at the water's edge, or the curious pelicans and majestic ospreys nesting on the channel pilings, there was no shortage of amusing incidents, such as an old boat on a mooring abruptly sinking, or someone flooding their boat as they tried to replace a through hull (while still in the water.)

In defense of my ignorance regarding the horseshoe crab, it actually *is* a prehistoric creature, since it is classified as a living fossil. I had never even heard of one before moving to Maryland, let alone seen one, so I was mystified by the alien looking carcass that I discovered one morning.

And with regards to flooding one's boat while changing a through hull, this too is apparently possible. You just need to be very fast, very efficient, and have the same sized fittings as you are removing. I would say that the last part of that statement is probably the most important factor as it was what caused the problem for the folks on dock B that day. The replacement part was too large to fit, and they hastily had to replace the original.

Suffice to say, I took to living aboard our boat like a duck takes to water (of which there were plenty of examples to observe, from the American Black Duck to the Common Goldeneye and even once spotting a Hooded Merganser). I simply loved the variability of our new home. Every day it was something new.

I was even happy with our shared facilities in the marina, such as they were. A communal shower block is not for everyone, but it was not the first time I had experienced such so I was perhaps a little better prepared than some. In fact, when I was younger I had an interesting experience while travelling in Europe.

Interlude, October, 1991

I had somehow managed to fall asleep on the crowded, noisy train. When I finally awoke I was pleased to see that the train was pulling into the station. We had arrived in Prague!

I looked through the grimy carriage window fully expecting to see the incomprehensible Czech language adorning signs and buildings. Oddly, it looked rather like German to me.

I gave a mental shrug, not knowing much about the Czech language at that time and disembarked with everyone else, hoisting my guitar case and backpack with practiced ease over my shoulder. I was still using the surplus Russian army torture device that I had traveled with through so many countries by then, but I had modified it with some additional padding on the straps. Now it was merely uncomfortable rather than having the potential to cause lasting physical deformity.

As I stood on the platform, I finally became aware that the language spoken by the tinny voice squawking over the public address system *was* German. Clearly, I was not in Prague after all. I began to get an uneasy feeling.

Without any clear idea of where I was, I made my way out of the station. As always, I walked with purpose, never minding the fact that I had no idea where I was going.

I had almost no money and I did not know anyone in the city. Which city, quickly became apparent; I was in Berlin. *East* Berlin.

Like many newly arrived penniless visitors, I gravitated to that part of the city that was poor, unregulated and the habitual home of hustlers, hippies and the homeless.

Not knowing what else to do, I stopped in a café and ordered "schwarz tea mit milch" (my German is not too good, but they got the message) and I took it to a small, rickety table by the window. With my trusty backpack and guitar next to me, I took stock of my situation.

My plan to stay in a cheap student hostel was clearly not going to work. I had no idea if such things existed in Berlin and if they did I had no idea where.

I had made a booking to stay in a youth hostel near the center of Prague's historic district. It was cheap, basic, but at least I could afford it. Now, I would have to take the train back to Prague if I was going to continue with that plan.

But I was in Berlin! I had not planned to be there, but now that I was, I found myself warming to the idea of spending a few nights in the city. All I had to do was figure out a real cheap place to stay. I considered my options.

A hotel was out of the question, and I didn't know anyone I could couch surf with in spite of the fact that I had previously dated a young woman who hailed from Berlin. However, we broke up under difficult circumstances (in the Lybian desert at a tiny oasis would you believe) and she went back to her girlfriend (which came as a big surprise to me, I can tell you). I was quite sure that my suddenly turning up on her doorstep would be met with zero enthusiasm. Especially from her girlfriend!

I wondered if my best bet might be to try to earn a little money through busking. Although I can play well, I can hardly sing. Any money I earned would be from pity, not appreciation of my talent.

At that moment, someone interrupted my thoughts with a question.

"Kann ich ihren tisch teilen?"

I looked up at a strangely dressed young woman with dreadlocked hair, large floppy hat and battered suitcase in one hand and coffee mug in the other. My ability to speak her language was limited to a few phrases and I replied that I did not understand.

"I said, can I share your table?" She repeated in flawless English.

I nodded and pulled my guitar case out of her way. The café had filled up while I was musing over my options and it was clear as I glanced around that there were very few places left to sit.

"Of course. Please join me."

"Danke." She sat down, and pulled out a tin box which she opened. Inside was loose tobacco and a packet of Rizla papers. She proceeded to deftly roll a cigarette. When it was done, she offered it to me. I shook my head, and she put it to her own mouth, lighting it with a match from the book on the table.

There was no ash and surprisingly little smoke from her roll up. It was consumed in a matter of a minute and she dropped a tiny bit of still glowing white paper into the ashtray.

"My name's Mike," I said.

"Stella," came the reply.

During the next few minutes as we chatted, I relayed my comical predicament to Stella. She laughed as I described my confusion when I realized that I was not in Prague. Then, she offered me a lifeline.

"If you need a place to stay, you can use my wagon."

"Your wagon? What's that?"

Now, I am not one to normally look a gift house in the mouth, but I did not understand what she was referring to. How does one borrow a wagon?

"What kind of wagon?" I asked, not unreasonably.

"The road workers have these little huts on wheels. You know, for when it rains. Wagons. I have one. You can borrow it for a few days. I'm going to visit my mother, so it will be empty."

"Oh, I see. Well, that would be amazing. Thank you!"

She pulled a pen from somewhere and wrote an address on the book of matches on the table.

"This is where I live. There are no street numbers, or anything. You have to look for the wagon with the star painted on the door."

She wrote something else; a series of three numbers under the street name. "I have a lock on the door. This is the code. If anyone asks who you are, just tell them you're a friend of mine. It's a pretty laid-back place."

I nodded. "Thank you, again. I had no idea what I was going to do."

"I know. I could see that. I think that's why I wanted to sit here. Make sure you were okay."

I laughed. "Am I so transparent?"

"Maybe only to me. I'm a witch."

I thought she was joking, but when I got to the street in Kreuzberg where her wagon was located I discovered that it was not just a star painted on the door but a pentagram. Perhaps she was a witch?

Stella's wagon was not the only one there. A small community of similar conveyances had formed in an area of wasteland between two high apartment buildings, and there were about a dozen of the little workmen's huts, each with its own resident character.

Once over their initial suspicion of me, the community were very welcoming. I played guitar with some of them and they gave me food. No one demanded anything from me, but they were all willing to share what they had. I was deeply touched by their generosity.

As my tiny little borrowed wagon was really just a bed in a box, there were very little facilities. The entire community made use of one of the nearby apartment buildings, which appeared to be an unregulated squat.

Previously it had been a state-owned building but was now in a gray state of ownership. People lived there without paying rent, without owning their apartment and without any obligation. It could not last, but during the confusion of the country's reunification they were making hay while the sun still shone.

It was not long before I needed to make use of their facilities. In fact, on the second day of my sojourn in Berlin, I had spent my time busking, trying to make a few coins for dinner.

I had been moderately successful strumming and quietly singing out of tune, so I bought a loaf of bread and some cheese and was quite content with that. But what I really wanted (needed desperately if the reaction of those people who wandered near me was any indicator) was a shower.

I asked one of my new neighbors and he explained. There was a shower block in the nearby apartment building that was open to anyone. Perfect.

I found it easily enough. It was empty when I arrived. Inside was a row of four showers (no dividers) and one standalone bath tub in the middle of the room plus a pair of sinks with broken mirrors above them on another wall.

I disrobed, piled my clothes into a corner, then got under the powerful shower and commenced to have a good scrub. I had been at it for a couple of minutes when the door opened and two women walked in.

"Oh! Sorry! I thought this was the men's shower," I sputtered, as I turned away from them in embarrassment. Realizing that they could now see my bottom in all its glory, I instinctively turned around, only to reveal even more of myself. I spun around again, my face burning.

One of the young women laughed as she pulled her T-shirt over her head. The other put a plug in the bath and started running the water. In seconds, both of the young women were naked and standing under the shower next to me.

This is not the start of a Penthouse letter. As attractive as those women were (and they were very attractive) it was far from an erotic experience. I was not used to such an open and casual attitude to nudity and I was completely unaware of the shower etiquette in what I quickly understood was an old-fashioned hippy commune.

So far, my life had completely failed to prepare me for this situation. I took a surreptitious peek (or two, or three) as I desperately tried to appear as if I was used to co-ed showering.

And if any potential thoughts of a romantic nature did occur, they were quickly dispelled by the arrival of a huge man who stripped down to his cowboy boots before jumping into the bath. He reclined with his booted feet sticking out of the tub. Then he lit a cigar and began to sing loudly and out of tune in German.

Even after a couple of decades of travel, I have never had anything like the same experience again. Still, I live in hope.

* * *

On Delphinus, we did not have the luxury of our own shower and though we did have a head, we tried to use the marina facilities as much as possible. Our boat was, to be honest, a little basic when it came to the creature comforts.

There was only one other liveaboard on our dock at that time, a guy named Steve. I had hung out with him a few times aboard his boat, a Hunter 27.

In fact, it was the very same one that we had first looked at when we arrived in town. Since Steve had acquired it (for a song) he'd really cleaned it up. It no longer smelled of mold and I was impressed at how much more space he had all to himself. However, his much newer boat seemed flimsy to me and in my estimation was not nearly as seaworthy as ours, so I considered that we had made a better deal with Delphinus.

I frequently compared every boat I saw to my own. And, so long as I did not stray too far from my dock A, I could maintain the pretense that Delphinus was the best. But as I ventured further into the marina, it was painfully clear that this was not so.

I suffered, as many of us do I am sure, from boat envy. This hit me very hard one day when I stepped aboard a rather large Nautor Swan, a 48-footer, belonging to an English couple doing the grand tour of the Caribbean.

I may have mentioned that I am physically of a rather large persuasion, so when I step on deck, the boat knows it. There is usually, depending on size and displacement, a precipitous rocking, or at the very least a gentle give, indicating that a person of 'substance' has stepped aboard.

I could have jumped up and down with a pogo stick on the deck of that Swan and it would not have even noticed. It was such a solid, heavy, and well-built vessel (weighing in at 36,000lbs, dry) that I fell instantly and horribly in love with it.

When I went back to my own little floating sea shack I was struck by just how much compromise I had made. I did not dare ask the Swan's owners how much they paid for their boat. Aside from the fact that this can be viewed as bad manners, I did not really want to know the answer. I was sure that the main winches in the Swan's cockpit cost more than we had paid for Delphinus.

The Swan's owners were a nice couple and I extended an invitation for them to stop by and visit, but they never did. Probably for the best. After viewing the sheer luxury of the Swan's interior, I felt very humbled about my own boat. From that point I did not judge Steve so harshly for his choice. At least he had a working shower!

But one thing I did learn from this event was that while I wished that I could have a bigger, better, newer boat, I did not actually *need* it. The fact is, we had achieved a major ambition and were beginning to experience the joys of sailing, all without spending more money than we could earn in a lifetime.

Delphinus might have been cheap but it would take us to the same places and provide the same view as that of a more expensive boat. I could not complain. Still, it would have been nice to have a bit more space. Just in case anyone popped in.

Not that we got too many visitors in the early days as we were a little secluded. Most of the liveaboards were over on Docks C and D. But if we had any doubts about getting to know the neighbors, our daughter didn't. She was a loquacious talker and drew attention wherever she went.

Kids from other boats would often turn up asking if she could come out and play with them. They were cruising kids, whose parents were shepherding them down to the Caribbean, or they were on their way back north, depending on the season.

It was always nice to see cruising families and many stopped off at the Marina to recharge their batteries (both literally and figuratively) and to catch up on much needed repairs.

Our daughter made friends with any kid she met,

regardless of their age, and she had a great time visiting other boats and going on picnics, swimming in the little pool in the marina, or just playing outside on the grassy areas.

I had taken a job in the marina (the commute was great!) working as an apprentice rigger. My boss' kids would often visit my daughter and they would cram themselves into the forepeak and play for hours with the stuffed toys that lived there.

Some of the liveaboards had pets, which also provided entertainment. Especially an old, fat cat, which my daughter loved to chase. Occasionally, it would let her catch it and then she would rub its belly while its purr rumbled like a New York subway train.

With so many visitors checking into the marina, there were always new boats to look at and I took every opportunity to examine them. Seeing so many beautifully appointed vessels spurred me on to make our own modest boat better, and as the weeks turned into months, we began to get Delphinus into shape.

There was one project that I simply had to tackle right away. If we were ever to actually get out on the water, the running rigging had to be seen to. This necessitated climbing the mast to 'thread the needle.'

If, like me, you are as lithe as an elephant on ice, then this can be a worry. Not only that, but I was mortally afraid of heights and always have been. I get the collywobbles walking across a bridge, or, heaven forbid, a glass walkway in the mall. Why on earth do they build those things?

Years later, I went to see the Grand Canyon, and like many, I thought that it would be a good idea to visit the Eagle Point glass bridge or 'Skywalk' as it is called.

Having paid a very stiff fee for the pleasure of inducing a heart attack, I felt obliged to actually try to inch my way out onto the bridge. I did so, and got about four feet out before realizing that I had nothing to prove to anyone and that retreat is the better part of valor. Hats off to the Hualapai tribe for their business acumen, but I won't be going back again.

The sensible course of action would have been to send my slim as a reed spouse up the mast, but since Kate was pregnant that was out of the question.

Luckily, Delphinus had mast steps. They were clearly home made, but also clearly functional having been cut from aluminum plate and bent to shape before being riveted to the mast. However, the edges of some of the steps were knife sharp. Care would be needed.

Climbing a mast, even with the help of mast steps is dangerous if you are not wearing a harness. But with no halyards to make use of, I had little choice in the matter. In spite of the lack of safety precautions and the fact that I was terrified, up I went!

The climb itself was not terribly difficult. Nor was feeding the halyards through the mast sheaves. I had tied the lines to my belt and dragged them up with me, which worked well. Note: If you have halyards with fitted shackles, be sure to feed the line through the sheaves in the correct direction. The last thing you need is to have to go back up and do it again.

I also had a few tools and some parts to work with, once I got to the top. The bigger task in this process was changing a bulb in the masthead light. This required extreme caution, as I needed both hands to perform the operation. The fact that this left me clinging to the mast by my thighs and sheer will power made for a few tense minutes. I removed the small screws that held on the lens and popped them into my mouth for safety. Then it was just a question of replacing the bulbs and refitting the lens.

If you have not actually clung to the top of a forty-foot pole, then you would be forgiven for thinking, 'big deal' right about now. But as the mast swayed alarmingly, no doubt due to the addition of a large weight acting as a counterbalance to the keel, I found myself calculating the odds of actually landing in the water rather than the deck or the dock when I inevitably fell.

I had in mind those circus acts where crazy individuals will swan dive from a high point into a tiny tub of water. The record for this was set in 1948 when Roy Fransen dived from 110 feet. His achievement remained unbroken for 49 years. Sadly, while performing his 'Dive of Death,' Roy actually did die. As it turns out, his act was aptly named.

Not wanting to follow in his footsteps, I got the job done and came down, exercising the same extreme caution, with a grim smile of triumph and a justified sense of accomplishment. As boat jobs go, this was relatively low on the expertise scale, but nevertheless I felt proud and just a little saltier as a result.

We now had running rigging and we wasted no time in hanking on our sails and doing a practice raise, while still in the slip. The sails went up, and the sails came down. Job done!

Since we did not have a roller furling, we kept the Genoa bagged in the forepeak when not in use. There is no need to let it weather if we were not going to need it. This was a handy tip from Steve, and in spite of his also being something of a sailing noob, he was a font of practical advice, often passing tidbits our way.

When I mentioned that the topping lift line was 'grubby' he told me to wash it. I laughed, thinking he was joking, but his solution was to put it in a pillow case and throw it in the washer next time we did a load of laundry. We did. It came out looking almost new. And the softener really made a difference!

After that, we always put running rigging or even dirty dock lines in the washing machine. The secret is the pillow case. It stops the line getting too tangled and jamming up anything inside the machine. Note. Do not leave any shackles on if you do this. The noise is prodigious.

Each new task that came our way was met with the same degree of caution and naive enthusiasm. This included restoring the teak planks in the cockpit, which transformed the look to such a degree that I cannot understand why people prefer to let them weather. I much prefer the warm golden brown of oiled teak over the dirty gray when it is neglected.

We also repainted the deck, which, like a facelift and tummy tuck, took years off our boat. With this done, we then added a rather nice non-skid pattern (we used fine sand mixed into the paint which worked amazingly well) by judiciously taping the deck, painting it, then removing the tape.

With the companionway hatch varnished and shore power and a telephone landline hookup installed, plus a host of other jobs done, the boat had gone from a diamond in the rough to a shining rock that Elizabeth Taylor would be proud to own. Needless to say, the first weeks were very busy but eventually there was nothing else for it but to take Delphinus out and raise a sail. It was time to learn what our boat could do!

The day we decided to go was when we discovered that the Chesapeake has a very curious feature. Not only is the bay tidal, which means the depth of water under the keel can vary by as much as six feet, or several meters, but when a strong wind blows in the same direction as the current then the bay practically empties and boats end up sitting on the mud.

We found this to be the case the next morning. The

boat was so low in the water that the dock lines were stretched practically to breaking point. I had to release and retie them. In fact, the dock was just above my head height when standing on deck. I found that if I stood on the push pit, I could just about scramble up onto the dock. My much shorter and pregnant wife could not. We needed to borrow a ladder in order to get her off the boat.

Note to self: Add a small, folding stepladder to the boat's inventory and learn how to read a tide table.

Chapter 10 – Transferable Skills

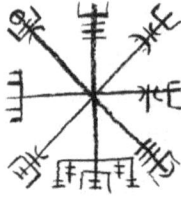

"An investment in knowledge
pays the best interest."
~ *Benjamin Franklin*

In chapter 5, 'How to Afford a Boat,' I touched on one of the transferable skills that I brought with me when living aboard; this was mechanical know how, in particular with cars.

Automobiles may not appear to have a lot in common with boats, since generally speaking they do not float and there are a lot less sails involved, but appearances can be deceptive. Aside from the obvious fact that both conveyances have an engine, they also comprise sophisticated electrical systems, with batteries, fuses, alternators and a good number of belts and pulleys.

We'll get back to that in a moment: First, a little anecdote.

When I first started contemplating life afloat, I thought that I would need to do a lot of research and reading and learning before even setting foot on a boat. I bought a book of knots and tried to teach myself. I read Chapman's Piloting & Seamanship end to end.

I bought other books, including some on unlikely

topics such as storm tactics. Basically, I spent a lot of time faffing around not getting much done because I was so busy trying to learn everything all at once.

This is a mistake. Don't assume that you have to be an expert on everything. First of all, there are a lot of people who will always know more than you, on any topic, so don't sweat it. Do not try to pass yourself off as an old salt. It is not necessary, and you will quickly make a fool of yourself.

There is no shame in admitting that you do not know something, and there is no shame in admitting that you need help.

I ask for help all the time. If I cannot do something, I have no problem finding someone that can teach me. This is a strength, not a weakness. Ignorance is only a problem if you prefer it to asking someone for assistance.

Get used to asking advice. If the person you asked does not appear to know, or is just a grumpy old fart, don't worry. There are plenty of other people who will be more than happy to pass on a few sage words, or relate their personal experience using this product or that tool, or whatever.

So when it comes to the 'water related bits,' don't worry if you do not know everything. That being said, take comfort in the knowledge that you already know a lot of things that will help to prepare you for your sailing future.

The following is a list of recommendations for things that you can get to grips with before moving afloat, assuming you have not already mastered them. Many of these are likely to be familiar to you. If you have owned your own home, most likely you have taught yourself how to fix much of it. Being handy around the house is a very good attribute and suggests that you will be handy on your boat too.

If you do not already have one, I recommend that you get a multimeter and learn how to use it. This will prove to be a highly useful skill that you will rely on again and again as you try to debug electrical faults.

And talking of electrical issues, a key skill is knowing how to solder. Connecting two wires is more than just twisting the ends together and taping them, or even worse, using a wire nut. A good, long lasting join that will resist corrosion, as well as the motion of the boat is important, no matter what system you are working on, so this is a highly useful skill to master (and, let's be honest, not a difficult one.)

These are all transferable skills, since the same methods can be used on a car or motorcycle as well as a boat.

In fact, everything you learned while working on your father's Chevy can be applied to your boat. The care and feeding of an internal combustion engine is much the same, even if marine engines are a little different.

For example, when fitting a new oil filter in my car, I always add a little oil inside of it, and then wipe a little more around the sealing edge with the rubber gasket before tightening it in place. I do exactly the same thing on the oil filter on my boat's engine.

It should be noted that marine engines have multiple filters for various things (air, oil, fuel, raw water) so when servicing your engine, make sure you get them all.

There are a hundred tips and tricks that I could mention here, but you probably know most of them already as what works for your land yacht will likely work just as well on your boat too.

These are all tips that I picked up during my first days riding a motorcycle and then driving a car. Even though I knew nothing about mechanics, and had no one to teach me, somehow I had managed to pick up some basics, and this gave me the confidence to try to resolve any problems that arose.

Interlude, May 1981

The bike felt sluggish during the ride home. It was definitely getting slower, less responsive. Not to mention the black cloud of smoke emitted from the exhaust. This was not the first time this had happened, and I had an idea what was wrong with it.

I pulled into my road, drove up onto the garden path belonging to our little house, then kicked down the side stand. Once the engine had cooled enough, I would get to work.

I went inside to fetch my tools. They were not much to look at. A plastic bag containing a motley collection of wrenches and screwdrivers, a small hammer and the pride of my collection, an impact driver.

For this job, I would need my spark plug wrench. It was a cheap tool, made from mild steel and prone to rusting, but it did the job.

It only took a minute to discover that the spark plug was, as expected, fouled. There was a thick, oily black coating over the ground electrode. Squatting down on my haunches, I scraped the plug end along the stone that edged the pathway leading to the front door.

I scraped the plug back and forth until the bottom shone like new. That was not going to fix it though. The other side of the electrode was still covered in carbon and oil. I rummaged in my tool-bag and produced a well-used copper brush. A few good swipes with it and the spark plug was fine. Or was it?

I held the spark plug up and eyed it critically. The gap between the ground and center electrode looked too wide. I didn't have a set of feeler gauges, but it definitely looked too wide.

I tapped it on the concrete path until the gap approximated what I estimated to be the correct size. Thankfully, Japanese engineering had sufficient tolerance to allow for such slapdash maintenance.

Now satisfied that the plug was in tip top shape, I carefully threaded it back into the cylinder head. I made it finger tight, then used the plug wrench to snug it down. This was where you had to be careful. If you over tightened, then the thread could strip. I put the HT lead plug cap back on and I was done.

With the ignition turned on, I folded out the kick-start lever and gave it a solid kick, simultaneously opening the throttle wide. The bike caught and revved, the sound deeper and louder than normal since I had recently removed the baffles from the exhaust.

I smiled, and reduced the revs until the bike was ticking over. It almost stalled and I was forced to tweak the throttle to keep it running.

I would have to adjust the idle speed. I turned a screw on the carburetor body, and the engine picked up, running faster, enough to not stall. Perfect. I put my tools back in the plastic bag and threw them into the house.

There was still more smoke from the exhaust than I would like to see, but that would mean messing with the oil pump. Get that wrong and the engine would seize. Better to err on the side of caution even if it did mean having to clean the spark plug from time to time. I put on my helmet. It was time to ride.

* * *

If you have ever had a two-stroke motorcycle, the

good news is that the same problems you experienced on your bike will likely occur on your tender's outboard motor too.

This includes fouled spark plugs, no doubt due to an incorrect mixture (fuel and oil) as well as dirty air filters, flooding or dirty carbs, etc. If you have ever owned a Kawasaki triple, you are all set for maintaining your outboard. Also, you automatically get additional cool points for having bought a 'widow maker' as those bikes were known.

So far, this has all been about mechanical or electrical knowledge, which can be useful aboard a boat. But there are many household skills which can be transferable, not least of which is sewing.

Sails rip and need to be repaired. So do cushion covers and Bimini tops, etc. Practically any canvas item on the boat will need a little extra stitching from time to time.

On Delphinus, we made our own main sail cover, as well as winch and binnacle covers. Not only did this save money, but it ensured that if we needed to repair any of the items, we were in a position to do it.

Even the most mundane of household skills can find a place on your boat. Take, for example, painting. Taping up window frames so you do not get paint on the glass, and then painting with brush and roller both have application on a boat.

When the deck on Delphinus had become so worn that it was difficult to know where the non-skid had been, we set about painting it with Interlux's Hatteras Offwhite, then taping a pattern into it before applying new non-skid, which we made from Interlux Grand Banks Beige with fine sand added. The net result looked amazing, provided additional safety and increased the value of the boat.

We used the same skills that we had learned while

painting our apartment. This is the 'roll and tip' method where you apply the paint with a foam roller, and then 'tip' the paint, which is to say, smooth the paint with a brush.

There are a host of useful skills that any average home mechanic, or do-it-yourselfer will have, all of which can be applied to your new home.

If you have ever repaired a puncture on a bicycle inner tube, then guess what? Yep. it is the same approach to fixing a hole in your rubber dinghy. That being said, in my experience, they tend to leak more along their seams than from small holes, but you get the point.

Having a practical, hands-on attitude will help in the engine room, the galley, the salon, on the dinghy and in a dozen other areas. So don't underestimate yourself or your abilities. Far from coming to your boat unprepared and ignorant, you may already be far more capable than you give yourself credit for.

Chapter 11 – Shipshape and Bristol Fashion

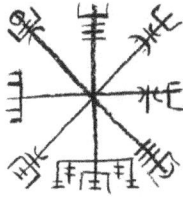

"We are tied to the ocean. And when we go back to the sea - whether it is to sail or to watch it - we are going back from whence we came."

~ John F. Kennedy

There are a thousand and one tasks necessary to perform in order to get a boat ready for open water. Amazingly, there are a similar number if you merely want to liveaboard, tied to the dock.

When we talked about changing our lives, we had modest ambitions. Buy a boat, put it in a marina, learn its systems, learn how to sail it, and slowly adjust from a liveaboard to a cruising lifestyle. It was a good plan.

But to make a sailboat a comfortable home for four people (daughter number two would soon arrive) much needed to be done, and mostly that meant spending money, something that I instinctively try to avoid. There seemed to be an almost endless array of items that either required attention, replacement, modification, or simply needed to be purchased because we did not have it.

I started with the essentials. Getting power to the boat. Since we planned to liveaboard full time, we wanted all the same amenities as we would have in a house, more or less. This included a television, a computer, a telephone, an electric heater and even a microwave oven. Obviously, this was going to be too much for the boat's batteries and an inverter, so I had either the option of an expensive generator, or connect the boat to shore power. Clearly, this latter was the better choice for us, as we were not close to being ready to go offshore.

I wired Delphinus for main's power. Since we were in the US, this was 120 volts. I installed a stainless steel 30 Amp inlet in a protected space in the cockpit. This was then wired to a breaker box and a Blue Seas' control panel, which I fitted inside the cabin by the nav station. I also installed outlets throughout the salon. With the addition of 12-volt lights which ran off the battery, we needed to charge our 'house bank,' so I installed a 3 stage, 15-amp battery charger too.

This enabled us to keep our batteries in tip-top shape, while taking advantage of all the power we would need while 'hooked up.'

In addition, we purchased a cheap, two element, electric hot plate, which fitted neatly on the gimballed gas stove.

Care with power consumption was required when out sailing, but so long as we were in the marina we could comfortably use as much juice as needed, and we needed a lot.

During the hottest months of summer, we ran an air conditioner that I mounted in the companionway. It was a lifesaver. Both Kate and I appreciated having a humidity sucking, cold air blowing monster, and who cared if you had to climb over it to get in and out of the cabin?

Now that we had energy, the next thing on my list was fresh water on demand. I installed an inlet with a pressure regulator to the side of the coach roof, and fed that under the sink. With the addition of a cheap faucet, we now had running water. For good measure, I also installed a solid brass Fynspray lever-action hand pump, to bring water up from the boat's own tanks when we were on the hook.

I preferred this over an electric pump for several reasons. First, when you have to pump water by hand, you tend to only use what you need. When water is available via a pressure system or supplied via an electric pump, it is easy to use far more than you require.

My other reasoning was that it was both cheaper, and easier to install a manual pump than electric. There was one less electrical draw on the batteries, and one less thing to go wrong. Plus, it looked good in the galley.

An interesting facet of these changes, was that I had to put a number of holes into Delphinus. I was somewhat amazed at the thickness of the material I was drilling and cutting into. Everything was much more solid than I had expected. Clearly, early seventies boats were built to heavier specifications than Steve's much newer Hunter. I had helped him out by drilling a hole for a new depth reader, so I had firsthand experience on the difference between overbuilt and barely built.

Even though our two boats had almost the same beam, ours felt much narrower. Space was at a premium inside Delphinus while Steve seemed to have plenty and to spare.

The modifications I made to Delphinus made our lives more comfortable but they cost a lot of money, and that was a scarce commodity.

I was dismayed at the amount that a simple telephone cable rated for 'marine' use cost. In fact, pretty much anything we needed was considerably more than I had anticipated. For example, compare the cost of an air conditioner made for the RV or marine market to that for a house. Ouch.

With money running out, there was only one thing to do; I was going to have to get a job, and soon. Luckily, our friendly yacht broker, Fran, stepped in. She was not overly technical and had all sorts of issues dealing with her laptop. I put on my consultant hat, and soon enough I was working in IT again, fixing computers. That paper MCSE was earning its keep!

Word got around in the marina, and I was approached by several people who asked me to design or extend websites. I even made one for a local brokerage. These days, it is a simple matter to create a website, since there are a good many powerful products available which make it easy, even for non-technical individuals. But this was 1999, and WordPress and similar did not yet exist.

For coding, I used Windows Notepad. It is not very high tech, but it did the job! The offer of work was certainly timely, and it kept us afloat (metaphorically) but it did not pay a lot, and I needed something a little more permanent.

As luck would have it, I heard of a local rigger who desperately needed to hire someone. As an Australian national, Bruce (all Australian men are called Bruce. No one knows why) needed to hire a US citizen in order to do business.

His workshop was very close by, so I went to see him. We had a quick chat.

"Okay, Mike. I'll take you on. But you're sure you have an American passport? You sound like a Pom."

"Well, I was born in Chicago," I replied. "But I grew up in England."

"Well, that's great. I need a US citizen as an employee. But the fact is, you're a bit crap. I'll have to let you go as soon as I can find someone better."

I nodded with a rueful grin at his estimation of my abilities. "No problem. I really am looking for something short term as it is. We're probably going to start cruising soon."

"Oh well, that's bonzo. Come by tomorrow, and I'll get you started."

In spite of my obvious failings, Bruce hired me on as an apprentice rigger, or rigger's mate. I was pleased as punch, and if he found someone better in a month or two, well, that was okay. At least I had a bit of an income for now.

As it transpired, it took six months before Bruce could find someone to replace me. And so, albeit temporarily, I had a job that paid a regular wage.

What does a rigger's mate do? For the most part, it was carrying things, hauling Bruce up the mast, and measuring things. But I did learn how to pressure swage the end fittings on standing rigging and how to splice an eye in braided line. Useful skills, which would come in handy one day, I was sure.

As an apprentice rigger, the wages were not great, but since I was pretty useless, I was happy to get anything. By now, we did not have any money left from our meager savings, so we lived on what I could earn. Consequently, wherever possible, I tried to find ways to minimize costs at 'home.'

This was a contentious issue between Kate and myself. While I was not willing to make allowances where safety was concerned, I saw no problem in using non-marine products, or materials on the boat, in non-critical applications.

A fact that you may well be acquainted with, the moment you apply the term 'marine' to anything, it instantly costs three times as much. This is why we had a household air conditioning unit, and not one designed for a boat. It performed exactly the same service, but at a fraction of the cost. So what if it looked a bit ugly?

As a dockside condo dweller, this worked out well. However, there are definitely times when you should not cut corners. An example is the wiring for the AC and DC control panels that I installed. I could have saved a few dollars by using standard wiring, but instead I shelled out the extra for 'tinned' copper wire.

Why is that important? Tinned wire is 'marine' grade. In essence, it resists oxidation longer, which, when it comes to wiring onboard a sailboat, is very important. I certainly thought so, since the last thing I wanted while out sailing was for the electrical system to suddenly fail due to a wire break, or worse, a fire caused by an electrical short.

Cleary, there are times when you should not try to save a few dollars by using the cheapest item. But equally, there are times when you can absolutely do so without compromising the safety or integrity of your boat.

This brings to mind a couple of incidents that Kate and I knocked heads over. Neither was worth the fight that developed, but living in a tiny space often leads to built up frustrations suddenly venting. If they did not, I would say that either you and your partner are saints, or a cataclysmic explosion is coming.

Anyway, back to the story. It all started when Kate said it would be nice to have a small table inside the cabin. Something to fit within our small salon space, that we could use for eating from and that would not be in the way when we made the bed up.

I said I would look into it, and try to come up with a solution. I already knew where I could get the wood.

There was a very nice piece of plywood just propped up against the rigging workshop where I spent most of my days. I asked around, and no one had any idea why it was there, or if it belonged to someone, so I snagged it.

The board was not marine grade plywood, but that did not matter to me. Since a small cabin table is not a critical system component, I believed that any old piece of board could do the job, so long as it was shaped, varnished and installed appropriately.

Kate disagreed, leading to the first of many discussions on the importance of marine grade materials versus non-marine.

As I recall, the conversation went something like this.

"Hey, check this out," I said, proudly presenting the off cut of plywood as I approached from the dock. "I found it by the workshop. I can make a small table for the salon from this."

Kate looked up from the cockpit where she was playing with our daughter as I stepped aboard.

"Is it marine grade?"

"No, but that doesn't matter," I replied.

"Yes, it does. You have to use proper wood," she insisted vehemently.

"Proper wood," I laughed. "Why?"

"Because!"

"What reason, aside from 'because' can you give for spending more on something, when I got a perfectly good piece of wood for free?"

I have always been willing to look in the nearest dumpster and see what I can upcycle. Kate interpreted this as my being 'tight,' or 'stingy,' or sometimes an 'ass-hat.'

I suspected that this was due to our different backgrounds. I grew up in poverty, while Kate was distinctly middleclass. What for her was false economy, was for me simple necessity. Needless to say, we had very different perspectives on some things.

Given our current financial situation, which could be characterized as dire, I was reluctant to give ground. Nevertheless, I skulked away with my prize, prepared to throw it in a dumpster before heading up to the chandlery to get a piece of 'proper' wood. But that is when lady luck smiled down on me. As I went to throw the redundant plywood away, I could not resist having a peek inside the dumpster first. And right then I made the fortuitous discovery of another suitably sized piece of plywood. But this one was stamped BS 1088.

That is marine grade plywood, guaranteed resistant to fungus, micro-organisms, heat, steam, cold water, boiling water and nuclear attack. I rushed back to the boat and like a cat depositing a dead bird at the feet of its owner, I delivered my prize to Kate.

"What's that?"

"Marine grade plywood. And enough to make a table."

Kate admitted that it 'might' do.

The plywood remnant was not very big, but I knew I could turn it into something useful. I took it to the workshop the next day, and during a slack period I cut it to shape. Over the next few days I sanded it, added teak fiddles and varnished it with half a dozen coats of clear. It looked great. If I had seen it in a chandlery, I could easily imagine that it would sell for big bucks. I was more than a little pleased with myself.

I kept it under wraps, so Kate did not get to see my progress until it was finished. I took it to the boat when I knew she was out, and I set about fitting it to the compression post. When I was done, I sat back and admired my handiwork. It looked good. Big enough to be useful, small enough not to get in the way when we wanted to sleep and the wood's grain looked great, thanks to the varnish.

Pleased with myself, I waited for Kate's return. Soon enough, I felt the boat rocking as Kate stepped aboard with the baby.

"Well, what do you think?" I asked proudly with a nod towards my creation as I took the young one.

Kate sniffed while critically examining the table. "It's small."

"So is the cabin," I replied, no trace of smugness in my voice.

"Why is it shiny?"

"I varnished it."

"Well, that will mean more work, won't it?"

"Not for a couple of years, I think." I had an answer for everything, and in the end, Kate had to admit it was a good job. Later that night, I saw her putting a beer mat under her glass, so as not to make a ring on the new table.

We used my dumpster table continuously for the next two years, and never had to varnish it again.

I chalked this up as a victory for the pragmatic, but the idea that everything had to be 'just so,' caused many conflicts between us. I will cheerfully admit that I have a very 'laissez-faire' attitude when it comes to, well, just about everything. But I believe that this is a strength, especially when it comes to boating on a budget.

This was something that not only Kate and I butted heads over. Some of the 'yachty types' who kept boats in the marina would look down their noses at anyone who did not coil their lines exactly right or did not remove their tender from the water, but rather let it drift behind their boat like a duckling faithfully following its mother.

I never did see eye to eye on the line coiling

nonsense, or on buying everything 'marine approved,' which I considered to be a wasteful and unnecessary extravagance that we could ill afford. However, there are times when retreat may be the better part of valor.

We needed some basic dinnerware; plates, cups, etc. My first instinct was to go to a garage sale and get everything we needed for a dollar. But, as Kate pointed out, the last thing we wanted was broken crockery everywhere.

I had to admit that made sense, so I suggested an alternate plan. We should look in Walmart. We could buy plastic plates, cups, etc, that would be perfectly suitable for us, and for a fraction of the price compared to the local chandlery. I was not concerned whether or not it was made specifically for boats, or had marine grade stamped on it anywhere.

But that idea met with resistance and we ended up getting high priced and rather ugly, so called 'marine suitable' dinnerware from West Marine.

It still looked like cheap plastic to me, but you have to pick your battles. Having recently 'won' an argument, I felt it best for marital harmony to now lose one. But I could take comfort in the knowledge that our dinnerware was fungus resistant and could withstand a nuclear attack.

But life aboard was not all arguing over the suitability of crockery. Even if there were plenty of discussions on how we could save money, there were some things that were simply better for us to do, than to pay someone else.

This is not just a desire to be frugal, but a concerted effort to be more effective and self-reliant. Both of which are important aspects of any cruiser's personality.

Since I had become a rigger's mate, however temporarily, I had developed some useful skills, and I was eager to apply them to our boat. The first thing we did was to make our own lazy jacks, which worked marvelously well. We also made our own sail and winch covers. We did not cut corners as we bought quality Sunbrella fabric. However, instead of getting it from a marine store, I went to a furniture upholsterer. Just because I wanted good quality, did not mean that I would pay through the nose for it!

Another major safety upgrade was the addition of netting all around the boat. Having lost our daughter overboard the very first day we set foot on a boat, we did not want to ever experience that again. Not to mention that we had another baby on the way.

So our daughter got used to wearing a harness and being clipped to a jackline when we sailed or she wanted to play 'topside.' The new netting added another layer of protection, plus, it helped give us that salty 'cruiser look' we so badly wanted.

As time progressed, Delphinus was transformed from an obscure sailboat into our home, and I began to feel that the life I wanted for my family was not only possible, but it was within our grasp. We were making progress. The boat was in good shape, we were learning to sail and it was only a matter of time before we set off on our grand adventure.

But first, I had to take Kate to the hospital. Her labor had started.

Chapter 12 – A New Shipmate

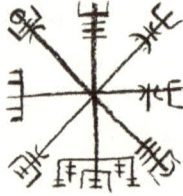

"There is nothing--absolutely nothing--half so much worth doing as simply messing about in boats."
~ *Kenneth Grahame*

We had been living aboard for perhaps six months when our new shipmate arrived. I do not remember anything at all about her birth, which is strange, since I was there at the hospital and was active during the delivery. Did I cut the cord? I don't know. Selective amnesia, maybe? Possibly PTSD?

Whatever the reason, while I may not remember too much about the details, I was thrilled with the outcome.

Daughter number two came home with us after a few days, and was immediately inducted into the crew. Her job was to look cute and gurgle. However, while our new shipmate was beautiful, she was also noisy and smelly (no doubt taking after her father) and on a small boat that is a challenge. But we adapted and made the best of it.

Having a toddler onboard a boat is hard, but with a newborn it is even more so. Everything that you do in a house with a baby is much harder on a boat. But having said that, at least our boat came with a built-in baby changing station.

The chart table, big enough to hold a fully unfolded admiralty chart, was also big enough to hold a baby, so that was handy. Dirty diapers would be sealed into plastic bags and tied off, before being deposited into the cockpit. Anyone leaving the boat had the responsibility of removing these and disposing of them in the garbage containers on shore.

We were the only couple with a baby living in the marina at that time, although not long after, a Swedish couple arrived in a 30-foot Vindo, with a baby only slightly older than ours. They had just crossed the Atlantic with their little bundle of joy, so hats off to them for their daring!

Vindo boats have a great reputation (something about Scandinavian built boats demands respect. Is it a Viking thing?) and older Vindos often sell for more than much newer boats from lesser makers. Ferenc Máté, a knowledgeable sailor and a particularly favorite writer of mine, said of Vindos that "the workmanship is so precise that a violin maker wouldn't improve on it."

I can attest to that. Their boat was beautiful and had made the Atlantic crossing without mishap. They did not stay in the marina long though, as they just needed to resupply before heading south. I will admit, I felt bitter envy that we were not doing the same. But a new baby takes a lot of looking after and Kate was adamant that she was not going anywhere out of range of quality medical facilities.

I could not argue with that point of view as nothing is more precious than a child, and like any father I would do anything to ensure that my kid was well taken care of.

Unfortunately, that is when things got difficult. Obviously, having a baby is a wonderful thing, but it had a serious impact on Kate. She had suffered from postpartum depression after our first was born, but that was nothing compared to what happened to her now. It is normal for women, and indeed some men, to become depressed after a birth, but this typically clears up as hormone levels adjust and the woman's body returns to its pre-pregnant state. However, Kate seemed to be hit much harder this time around.

I would have liked to be more available for Kate, but in the final days of her trimester I got fired from my local rigging job and that meant no more hanging around in the marina.

The parting of the ways had long been expected, So I was not surprised when a handsome, tanned young man showed up at the workshop one day, marking the end of my time in the boating industry.

I made him a coffee, and we chatted while waiting for my erstwhile boss to arrive.

My 'firing' was entirely amicable, and we had a good laugh over some of my antics while working for Bruce. There were no hard feelings on either side as the arrangement had benefitted us both.

But now that I needed another job, I was finally willing to accept a call to come back to the world of computers. We had been scraping by on a pittance for the last half year and I felt that it was time to make some real money.

I reasoned that we could save for a year, maybe two, then we would be able to do some serious cruising and really begin to experience what the boat had to offer.

Knowing that we needed good medical coverage, I had taken a job with an IT consultancy in Bethesda. This is a suburb of Washington D.C., and it is a center for high tech companies.

The medical coverage was great, as we did not have to pay a penny for Kate's time in hospital, or the subsequent checkups that come hand in hand with having a baby. However, the flipside of that was I was away far more than when I had worked for Bruce as his rigger's mate, and there was no popping by the boat to say "Hi" during the middle of the day.

In spite of the good pay and the great health insurance, it was not all hunky dory. There was little or no paternity leave granted by most companies in the US at that time. And as progressive as my high-tech IT company liked to portray itself, it was no exception. I was given a day off for the birth itself (compassionate leave) and one more day in addition, *which I could take when needed.* I had to laugh when I saw the email from HR.

Two days leave are not much when you are dealing with a newborn, and Kate and I were both acutely aware that she would inevitably be left to do everything since I was away as much as twelve hours a day. She felt overwhelmed, which is not surprising, and suggested that we place our oldest into a part time daycare so she could give the necessary attention to our new shipmate.

To me, this seemed the height of folly. Kate had argued for the chance to be home with the kids in order to provide the best upbringing possible. And now here she was trying to foist our oldest onto someone else. I did not like it. And yet, I could see that Kate was worn out and a good night's sleep was not going to fix it. She needed help, and I did not know what else I could do, except maybe quit work and stay at home with her. Unfortunately, this was not an option. Even though were living in a boat, and should therefore have much less expenses, we had once again fallen into the trap of spending precisely as much as we earned.

Spending creep is probably the biggest challenge

you will face when trying to save for your boat. And even though I now had a job that paid well, somehow we still managed to spend pretty much everything I made and there were no savings to tide us over while Kate weathered the storm as her body adjusted.

So, daughter number one went to daycare for part of the day. I would drop her off in the morning and Kate would collect her in the afternoon. In some regards, this might have been a blessing, since it ensured that Kate would walk a couple of miles each way, pushing the baby carriage. Exercise is known to be beneficial to depression. Perhaps it helped. I hoped so, because nothing I did appeared to make a difference.

The dream of living a life less ordinary was still very much alive, even though I had succumbed and returned to the rat race. To be honest, it felt as if I had allowed myself to be plugged back into the Matrix, but I consoled myself with the knowledge that now we could afford a windlass and a bigger anchor.

And our new crewmate was a delight. She quickly learned to climb the netting I had installed to keep her from rolling out of her bunk. First, she would grab the top of the netting and drag herself up to a standing position. Then she would cock one leg up, before flipping herself over. At that point, it was a simple process to climb down the other side. All this before she had even learned to crawl.

Now that we had two kids to keep an eye on, sailing became an even rarer event, but that was okay. I figured that we would have plenty of time for really learning the ropes when the girls got bigger and we started to actually cruise.

We did take the boat out from time to time, while our youngest was still too young to crawl. We kept her securely strapped into her car seat, wedged at the bottom of the companionway so we could keep an eye on her from the cockpit. She was on the centerline at the lowest point on the boat, and was therefore the most stable. She slept most of the time and our system worked like a charm.

One particular trip was rather memorable. We were running the main and genoa when it started gusting hard. We were being overpowered, so we took down the genoa. Even with just the main, we were heeling something fierce. But Delphinus was flying and I really got a feeling for what a good, solid boat she was.

Coming off the waves, she would momentarily hang in the air, then crash down with a terrific splash of spray, some of which would reach us back in the cockpit.

I was a little scared and kept thinking that I should round up and put a reef in, but the speed and the spray were exhilarating and I was full of a wild longing to just keep going. But we were on the bay, not the ocean and it was getting dark. I turned the wheel and spilled the wind, before dropping the main and heading home for Back Creek using our iron genny, the single cylinder thumper.

It was the first time we had buried the rail and it was more fun than I can ever remember having. For me, that was what it was all about. Sailing with my family in a good strong wind with six-foot waves. Even in the protected waters of the Chesapeake it felt like adventure. If only we could do more!

From that day, I looked for excuses to go out on the water. When someone said they were going for a sail, I would ask if they wanted a crewman. When there was a race, I volunteered to change sails.

It is easy to go sailing when you just need to slip the lines. On Delphinus, we practically had to spend a full day in preparation, getting things organized, put away, moved ashore to a locker, and generally shipshape before we cast off.

Kids on a boat complicate matters extremely. Their physical wellbeing takes precedence over all else, so one parent is always on child watch, while the other sails the boat. This is a reasonable distribution of labor. At least, until you need to change a sail or do some other task that requires someone at the helm and someone on deck.

But even with our inbuilt constraints, we managed to get out on the water from time to time, enjoying the sunset far from shore.

If the kids kept us from going sailing as often as we wanted, at least they were not the reason that we ran into problems when we did. Poor decision making and a lack of experience were our real problem, and that latter could only be cured by more trips, not less.

Of course, it is not as if every outing we made in our boat resulted in disaster. It just seemed that way. And if a disproportionate amount of our trips were marred by issues, they were always of our own making. We simply did not know enough to know that what we were doing was dangerous.

They say that the sea is a harsh mistress. We were going to find out just how true that statement can be.

Chapter 13 – When Things Go Wrong

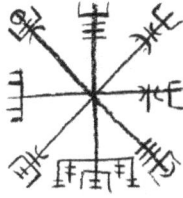

"He wrongly accuses Neptune,
who makes shipwreck a second time."
~ *Publilius Syrus*

Even experienced sailors will make mistakes. In the worst cases, this can end up costing lives, which is terrible. For the most part, thankfully, it simply causes embarrassment. When it came to noobs like Kate and myself, we were acutely aware of the potential for problems and were constantly aware that everything we did could be a danger to ourselves and others. Sometimes extra vigilance paid off, and sometimes it didn't.

While in the process of anchoring in a sweet little cove we'd found, we had a little snafu. The dinghy's painter became entwined around the prop. Since we did not have a windlass I was at the bow letting out the rode and tying it off. Kate was at the helm, backing up, digging in the anchor. Unfortunately, she neither heard my yells nor noticed when our dinghy drifted around to the stern. The painter became submerged (why did we not use floating line?) and it immediately wrapped itself around the prop. Naturally, this became a problem. Luckily, Kate saw what had happened, and shut off the engine before any real damage was done.

But the solution to any problem is the right attitude. We appeared to be anchored well enough, so now that we had accomplished that task, it was time to deal with the next problem. Unwrap the line fouling the propeller.

"Someone will have to go down and free the line," I said with a nod to the murky and most likely chilly water.

"Yeah," came the reply as Kate handed me a face mask and a look of sympathy.

"Uhm, rock paper scissors?" I countered.

"No need. Here, hold this," she replied, handing me a waterproof flashlight.

Aside from my aversion to heights, another tiny phobia of mine is not being able to see what is below me when swimming. Once, while in the Red Sea snorkeling above a reef, I came to a drop off point where the reef plummeted into the dark depths. I floated above it and all I could see (thanks to my fervid imagination) were things with sharp teeth and tentacles looking back at me.

My heart nearly stopped in abject terror, and I swam back to shore, possibly breaking several speed swimming records. Needless to say, there was nothing down there, but the imagination does not work on logic.

Of course, that was years ago and far away. I was older and wiser now, and this was not the Red Sea. So I reluctantly got ready to dive down below the boat. I was sure that there were no monsters in the Chesapeake Bay and yet I could not help but remember the poem of the ancient mariner and the line 'slimy things that did crawl with legs, upon the slimy sea.'

Even so, over the side I went. The water was indeed

chilly, but not too cold to work. Certainly not less than 60 Fahrenheit or around 15 centigrade. Naturally, the flashlight did not actually work under water, even though it was supposed to, so visibility was close to zero. I came back up, gave Kate the light, and asked for a knife. I would have cut the line free, while more or less blind.

I went back under, working my way down, finding my way by feel. With one hand holding onto the skeg, I tried to pull the rope free, and even tried reversing the direction of the prop, but it was too tightly packed.

I started to work, sawing away at the line. I could not stay down for long, not being a trained diver, so I had to keep going up for air, then returning to my task. Three times I had to return to the surface. On the fourth dive I was done. With lungs beginning to burn I got the last of the line cut free. Now I could turn the prop easily with my hand.

But I was out of air and getting desperate. I needed to surface and I came up fast, not realizing the dingy was directly above me. I hit my head on its hard bottom, causing me to black out. I was still under water, unseen and unconscious, slowly drifting down towards the bottom.

I could not have been out for more than a few seconds though. When I came to, I panicked. I was trapped, I was drowning, which way was up? Still under the dinghy, I turned, clawing, spluttering and coughing when I finally reached the surface.

I still had the knife, which amazed me. I passed it carefully up to Kate, trying to stay the shaking in my hands. She was totally unaware of the drama that had taken place just a few feet away.

I felt as weak as a kitten, and could barely climb the swim ladder. Even so, I felt pretty good about myself. I had conquered a primal fear, freed the prop, and we could make use of the engine again.

Once I had gotten my breath back, I set to the next task. Attaching a new painter to the dinghy.

"Can you get me that yellow line from the locker in the salon," I asked.

Kate went below to fetch the rope. She looked at me quizzically. This line did not float either, but I was damn well going to make sure we did not back over it a second time.

"I'll have to make a new painter," I said as I tied the dinghy off on the portside cleat with the now reduced length of line.

"Why is it called a painter?"

As a Norwegian, Kate's English was practically flawless, and if she did not know a word's meaning, it was because it was simply too obscure. However, she believed that I would know, since I was brought up in the English language.

"I have no idea," I replied, as I tied a bowline through a shackle. "Something to do with painting, obviously."

Of course, it wasn't anything to do with painting. I looked it up. Apparently, from around the middle of the eighteenth century, the line attached to the bow of a boat has been called a 'painter.' It derives from an old French word, and is originally from the Latin, 'pendere,' which means to hang. Pendulum and pendant originate from the same source.

As interesting as that fact is (or isn't) I was fully aware that freeing the prop shaft should not have been so hard. It was a red flag that I was far from ready to tackle the rigors that cruising would no doubt demand. But I was determined to make my dream a reality. Where there is a will, there is a way and so what if I might have drowned.

Getting stuck out in the middle of nowhere without

a useable engine would not phase some people, but having just started getting familiar with our boat, losing the auxiliary engine was akin to "Houston, we have a problem."

But even though I had managed to save our bacon in that one example, it would not be the last time we had to deal with a wrapped prop.

During one expedition, we damaged the shear plate, the connector between the shaft and the engine. This is a sacrificial component that is designed to break at a certain pressure so that the prop shaft itself does not become damaged. Essentially, it is like a fuse; it would blow before any real damage could be done to anything expensive.

Well, one day it did 'blow.' But this time it was not our fault. The prop had become entangled in some line that had been abandoned, left to float like a sinuous trap below the water line, waiting to ensnare the unwary.

Without the shear plate, we were dead in the water. Of course, we could have used our sails to get home, but that would have demanded a level of competence that we simply did not yet have.

And while I removed the line (you can be sure I was more careful with regards to the dinghy) there was nothing that I could do about the shear plate itself.

Plus, now that the shaft was no longer connected to the engine I worried about the possibility of it simply falling out of the boat. Could that happen? I was not certain, but I made sure to lash the prop shaft with multiple fail safes, just in case.

I wondered about the possibility of fashioning a 'make do' sheer plate from some scrap wood. But without power tools, it would have taken quite a while, plus, if it were not precisely balanced my replacement would likely cause oscillation. Any vibration in the shaft as it turns at high speeds could be disastrous, as it might damage the shaft, the stuffing box, the transmission, and potentially even sink the boat.

I knew enough to leave it alone, so I got on the radio and requested assistance from SeaTow. They were kind enough to send a motorboat out to our location.

Although the boat that turned up was relatively small, I can tell you that it was powerful since it practically had Delphinus planing over the water. It also caused spray to fly up from our stern, which naturally fell into our dinghy which we were pulling behind.

Now, it may seem obvious, but when you add water to an object that has no egress, the object will fill and become heavy. This is exactly what happened to the dinghy, and at some unspecified point that new painter that I had made broke and the dinghy was lost.

As soon as we became aware of this fact, I jumped on the radio and called the captain of our rescue boat. He turned us around, and we had a look for the errant tender, not expecting to be able to find it, since we had no idea where or when we'd lost it. Plus, it was a cloudy night, and therefore pitch dark on the bay.

The tow boat captain used a powerful flashlight to probe the inky water in all directions. Remarkably, he saw something. We had placed reflective tape on the sides of the dinghy which stood out if you shone a light on them. Although it was sitting lower in the water than it should, our tender was still floating, and I think, trying to make its way south. We pulled it aboard for the duration of the journey home. Lesson learned.

Aside from running over submerged or semi

submerged objects (one time I saw a small barrel barely afloat, like the type rum comes in, another time an actual shipping container), the other likely issue is running aground. Since the Chesapeake is tidal, a route that swings close to land would be fine one day, with 2-3 feet of water below the keel and the next you would be running into the mud and coming to an abrupt stop.

When this happened to us, I hopped over the side and tried to push the boat out, back along the channel that we had made in the mud with our fin keel.

Perhaps this can work if you are on a rising tide, but we were not. So, we settled in for a few hours, waiting for the tide to turn so we could float off.

Mud is not the worst thing to run aground on, but I knew that it is generally accepted as bad practice to run aground at all. Occasionally, a power boater would approach and ask if we wanted a tow. I thanked them, and said we would be fine. And we were.

The tide lifted the boat, we backed off with the engine, and motored home. A little late, a little red in the face, but we made it, and learned another valuable lesson.

In our time aboard our little sailboat we faced numerous challenges. But not all of them were sailing related. Sometimes, there were problems that flummoxed us while still being tied to a dock.

Having small kids on a boat, especially a baby, demands certain things, including a baby carriage, or pram. We had one. A nice tan colored carriage that we would leave tucked under a tree by a fence when not in use. One day, we left it out on the dock. Of course, we applied the brakes so it would not roll away.

I don't know why, but we forgot about it and left it there overnight. In the morning, when we poked our heads out of the boat, we discovered that it was gone.

Of course, we first thought that it must have been moved by someone. Perhaps one of the marina personnel had (rightly) objected to its being left on the dock? We checked with the marina office. They had not seen it.

"It's been stolen," Kate declared.

"No way. Who would steal it?" I replied with certainty.

"Well, what other explanation is there?"

And that was the problem, I did not have one. "I don't know," I admitted.

It was not stolen, I was sure. But no one had moved it, either. Being the super logical detective that I am, I deduced that when you eliminate all the possibilities, whatever remains, however improbable, must be the truth.

It had been windy during the night. I had been woken by the constant ding dinging of dozens of halyards against dozens of masts. Hmmm . . . windy. Carriage. Dock. Water.

Well, I guess Sherlock Holmes would not be needed. It was, as he would say, elementary. I deduced that the baby carriage had been blown over and had fallen into the bay.

I was quick to test my theory and I used a small dinghy anchor as a rudimentary grappling hook. I attached it to a line, and started to trawl the area either side of the dock. I threw the hook out, and dragged it across the bottom. As I worked, I attracted the attention of several people and soon had a small crowd watching with avid interest as I trawled the water around our slip.

On about my tenth try, I snagged something. I pulled. It moved, but it was heavy. I pulled harder, and strained. Hand over hand, I dragged something from the bottom. It was the carriage! Other hands reached down to grab it, and in moments we had it back on the dock.

But it was a mess. Full of water and blackened by mud, I thought that there was no way we were going to be able to use it again. Amazingly, there was a small fish in there, flip flapping around in distress. I tossed it back into the bay.

Now that I had the carriage back on dry land, I immediately got it wet again with a high-pressure hose. That took off most of the gunk, but it was never the same and it had a bit of a pong. Thankfully, we did not need to use it for too much longer and traded it in for a much smaller stroller. Needless to say, when we got back from a walk with the baby, we folded the stroller and put it in the lazarette.

Top tip. If you are going to have a baby and liveaboard a boat, your baby carriage will need a lanyard. Either that, or get yourself a grappling hook now. It will save time later.

In relating these anecdotes, I have made us sound a bit hopeless, and in some ways we were. Practically everything we had to do was new to us, and came with a learning curve. That being said, not every problem we had was actually our fault.

As fall turned into winter and the water started to freeze, we needed a small heater to keep us warm and toasty. I had considered a propane heater since we could use it when away from the marina. However, I opted for electric in the end because I had read that for every gallon of propane you burn, you produce a gallon of water vapor. Whether or not that is true, our boat had humidity problems already, thank you very much, and I did not want to make it worse.

I bought a small electric heater instead. This worked great and we were never cold, even when the temperature dropped to well below zero centigrade or

32 Fahrenheit. Of course, we are not talking about arctic conditions, but we did get plenty of snow, and the bay did freeze close to the shore. We even, on occasion, discovered that we were entombed by ice in our boat. Imagine not being able to open the companionway hatch? It was frustrating.

Our self-generated humidity, caused merely by breathing, was enough to create an icy seal that trapped us. This happened on a couple of occasions, necessitating our calling out for help through an open hatch, or getting on the VHF.

I pondered if I should make a pan-pan call, but figured it was not really *that* urgent.

"Uhmm . . . Anyone in the marina copy."

"Hey, yeah, this is Jock. Switch to channel 68. What's up?"

"Hi, jock. This is Mike on dock A. We're snowed in. Can you come down and dig us out?"

I swear I could still hear the laughter even after I ended the transmission.

But ice could be a serious concern, and not just for us. That same winter, one of our liveaboard neighbors' cats went walkies on the frozen bay, which was evidently not very thick at all, since the moggy went through the ice and was unable to get out of the water. This was no doubt due to him being a bit of a fat cat. But who am I to judge?

Luckily for him, his cries were loud enough to wake me, and I went out on the dock to investigate. I took a flashlight and shone it out onto the creek. It was not long before I could easily make out the bedraggled feline struggling to clamber up onto the ice shelf, and failing.

I knew whom the cat belonged to, and ran to rouse his owner. It was the ginger tom and there was only one like it in the marina, belonging to a chap named

Ivar. He was originally Polish, but had immigrated as a child. I pounded on his hull and within moments, I was leading my worried and very hurriedly dressed neighbor back to dock A. We went out to the end of the pier, and although we could see his cat, we could not see how we could safely get out to it. If the ice did not hold *its* weight, it would not hold ours.

"What are we going to do?" I asked.

Ivar looked at me, despair written on his face. "Kurwa! I don't know. Maybe we can throw a line out to him?"

"Right." I rushed back to Delphinus and found one of our longer docking lines. Kate popped her head up from the cabin.

"What's going on?"

"Ivar's cat is in the water," I replied.

"Oh no! What can I do?"

There was no way I was going to let Kate risk going out on the ice to save the cat. She would do it, I had no doubt, but I was not willing to let her take the risk. I attempted to divert her with another task.

"Put the kettle on. It's freezing out here!"

Like most people with an English heritage, when faced with an emergency, I believed that a nice cup of tea would make everything better.

I found our longest docking line, then hurried back to Ivar. He tied a knot into the end to help weight it, then swung it about this head before casting it out to the cat.

His aim was good, but the line fell short. He tried again, straining to lean out over the end of the dock. Still no good. The cat cried out, scrambling furiously. Now that it could see its owner it became even more vocal with its howls of anguish.

"How about we push a dinghy out?" I said.

Ivar shook his head. "No chance. Too heavy. What

we need is a way to spread the load over the ice."

I thought. Ivar thought. The ginger tom cried. It must be desperately cold. How long had it been in the water? Would it have hyperthermia?

Then I had it. I knew what to do!

I ran back to Delphinus and opened the lazarette. I pulled out our new, folding ladder. Since we had been stranded in the mud unable to climb off our boat, I had been waiting for a chance to use it.

I rushed back to Ivar and he instantly knew what I had in mind. He tied the docking line to one end of the ladder, then climbed carefully over the side of the dock, lowering himself onto the ice.

I extended the ladder to its fullest length, and passed it to him. He placed it on the ice, pointing it towards the distressed feline, then laid himself flat. Slowly he pushed the ladder ahead of him, feeding it out towards his pet.

Using a kind of leopard crawl, he made his way closer and closer, pushing the ladder ahead of him. There was an ominous crack. Ivar froze. I shone the light down at him, but could see nothing amiss. Another crack.

Ivar thrust the ladder out as hard as he could and it slid over the ice directly towards the soggy moggy. It did not look like the ladder was going to make it, then the last steel rung settled over the ragged gash in the ice and instantly the ginger tom clawed his way out of the frigid water.

Now that it was on the ladder, Ivar called, trying to tempt the cat to come to him, but it was too frightened to move, and only sat shivering. Ivar inched his way back towards the dock, until he was satisfied that he was on firm enough ice. Then he got to his knees, and pulled the ladder using the lined tied to the bottom. Much closer now, the cat leaped into his arms and

Ivar wrapped it in his jacket, zipping it up.

Then Ivar stood carefully and passed me the line. I helped him clamber back up to the dock, before pulling the ladder up. As I proceeded to fold the ladder, Ivar rushed back to his own boat. The cat needed to be dried and kept warm. Perhaps it was already too late. I made my way back to Delphinus and Kate and the kids, who were all awake. Kate handed me a welcome cup of tea.

As it turned out, the ginger tom made a full recovery. A couple of days later, I saw him out on the ice again, but luckily, he made it home on his own. For the life of me, I cannot understand why he kept going out on the frozen bay. Having just used up one of his nine lives, one would think that he would be a bit more careful.

Chapter 14 – Right Boat, Wrong Time

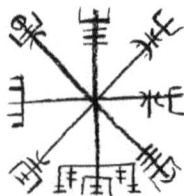

"If you find the will, you will find the way."

~ *MJ Kobernus*

When I first saw Delphinus, I knew that it had the necessary characteristics that I was looking for. It was a proven Blue Water sailboat, having successfully cruised the Caribbean by its previous owner for several years. It had an Aries self-steering rig, decent sails, oversized standing rigging and even though it lacked a water maker, it met the criteria that I had in mind for a safe, secure boat for me and my family. It was not very roomy, but you do not sacrifice seaworthiness for an extra cabin or a shower.

But as good as the boat was, that is where I made a huge mistake. I had bought a boat that would serve a *future* purpose, and likely serve it well, however, it was almost entirely the wrong choice for our initial needs at the time when we bought it.

One might think it only logical that getting a boat, living with it for a few years, and then cruising with it makes the most sense. The only problem with that plan is that we had to live with so many compromises within our narrow-beamed boat that before we came close to being in a position where we could go cruising we were more than a little frustrated and tired. Not only with the cramped conditions on the boat, but with each other too.

This is, after shortcomings with money, likely to be the biggest issue any cruising couple or family will deal with.

Frictions that you can learn to live with, or ignore when you have your own space to retreat to are suddenly magnified into major issues that cause flare-ups and arguments. This is particularly the case when you are practically sitting in each other's laps the whole time.

When we bought the boat we were naturally thrilled with her, but after several years of living aboard with two very small kids, the sheen had definitely worn off. It became hard work, and even though we did manage to squeeze in the occasional overnight adventure, my relationship with Kate began to suffer and I became concerned that we were destroying our marriage.

Far from living the dream, it seemed that we were killing it.

To me, the solution was to leave the dock, and face the daily challenges of cruising as a family. Shared adversity would bring us closer, I was sure. Plus the beauty of the places we planned to visit would make our petty squabbles pale into insignificance.

I will admit, I was naïve. Although I prefer to think of myself as a romantic. But my solution did not happen. We did not take off for unknown waters and share the wonders of the open sea. Why? What stopped us? I have thought long and hard on this question.

In my opinion, while the size of the boat was restrictive, it was sufficient. And after my working long hours for over a year in a tech company, we had enough money saved in order to sail away for at least

12-16 months, maybe more.

However, in the end there was one issue that I believe overshadowed everything else, depression. More specifically, I believe that it was post-partum depression.

I had seen some indication of this after the birth of our first child, but after the second arrived, there was little question in my mind that Kate had been deeply affected.

I will not pretend to be an expert. Nor am I an informed amateur psychologist. However, even with my basic and limited knowledge of motherhood and post-partum issues, it was obvious that Kate was subject to hormonal swings that affected her mood, and the way she spoke and acted.

We did not discuss it. Any effort on my side to bring it up was met with resistance, or blame. I did my best to accommodate Kate's needs, but since I was at work for long periods, she was forced to handle things with the kids on her own.

One of the most obvious issues that became apparent was that of privacy. Perhaps I had been too hasty in dismissing that tired old Hunter, the first boat we looked at with Fran. After all, it would have made a much better liveaboard. It had actual cabins, and a much bigger head, and, wonder of all wonders, the possibility of privacy. Sure, it needed a lot of work, but that was one area where we thrived.

Delphinus was in fine shape while we lived aboard. We had given her new running rigging, new wiring, painted the deck and the boot stripe as well as an almost endless list of upgrades that we tackled slowly and surely.

If I had to take one lesson away from my time with Delphinus it is this; space matters. Perhaps if we had made it to the Caribbean, maybe the compromises would not have been so difficult to live with.

If I could go back in time, I would make different choices. The first would be to go cruising in Delphinus and not give two seconds of thought if we could afford it or not. I should have trusted in the Universe to provide.

Alternatively, as we were still tied firmly to the land, then maybe buying a bigger boat that afforded more comfort would have been the smart move. Instead, we had a boat that, as much as I loved her, did not suit our immediate needs and which was never used for its intended purpose.

It was my fault. Mea culpa. I should have known better. But with no practical experience in living aboard, and no sailing experience, I had allowed my dreams to cloud my judgement. I had imagined that we could live in the boat for some years, then simply up anchor and go cruising.

People react differently to hardship and adversity. Some take it in their stride, while others struggle to maintain their composure, frequently allowing tiny issues to trigger eruptions of pent up frustration.

While we both tried to take a philosophical approach to the constraints of living aboard, it was Kate who struggled the most. I thought she could adapt as I had, but I was wrong.

"I want to go home," Kate said as she collapsed onto the salon sofa early one Friday evening. The kids were asleep in their bunks and we were settling down to watch a movie.

"Huh?" I replied, having not really heard, as I was fiddling with the VCR.

"I want to go home. To Norway," she reiterated calmly.

I looked at her, my brows beetling. "You mean you want to go on a visit?"

"No. I want to move to Norway. I'm tired, and it's just too much work. You're never here, and I have to do everything with the girls."

She sounded frustrated, angry. It was an old story, and one that has played out in many homes with many couples. And even though I knew how this story usually ends, I found myself following the traditional script written for the man.

"I can't help that I'm not here. I have to work, you know that," I replied more than a little defensively.

"I know. I'm not blaming you. It's just a fact. You're gone ten or twelve hours a day, and I have to look after the kids by myself."

"But you were the one who wanted to stay home with them. I wanted you to get a job and put the girls in kindergarten, but you said no."

"I know. And I am not saying that I was wrong, but it's just too much for me now. If we move back to Norway, at least my family can help out. They really want to."

"But that would mean that we give up everything we've been working for. No more boat. No cruising either. Don't you think we should do that first? Give it a year or two, then decide?"

Kate shook her head, tears forming. We talked about it during that weekend. By the following Monday, the decision had been made.

I could see that I was going to have to make a choice. Either, I could hold onto my dream, or I could hold onto my family. Those were the only two options open to me.

I never really did learn what Delphinus and I could handle at sea. Of course, we had taken her out in some interesting weather that had us flying off the waves. That was exciting, and I relished it, but those moments were too few and far between.

After only a couple of years, my dream of living aboard and cruising had come face to face with a reality I could neither avoid nor change.

As much as I was saddened by the situation, I could not give up on my family and I agreed to move to Norway. I understood that it was the end of my sailing career but I consoled myself by believing that perhaps there would be a new dream, something that we would both want as much as I had wanted this.

I was willing to begin a new life with a house and a mortgage. This was clearly what Kate needed, and I saw it as my duty to provide it.

Once again, we went through the process of selling and giving away whatever we could. Since we had so few material things now, it did not take long. Probably the only thing that caused me any heartache was selling my guitar, Blondie. I had owned it since I was 17, and it had traveled with me around the world. Selling it would be painful and I would surely never see its like again. After all, how many people have a guitar that has been played in Koln Cathedral, or on the streets of Berlin, or on a mountain in the Sinai or a desert oasis in Lybia? But now we needed every penny that we could get and I let it go, selling it to a co-worker for a very meager sum.

Moving from state to state within the US can be expensive, but moving from country to country is another magnitude of cost. Every penny counted. Even though Blondie was a part of me, I sold it on the strict condition that one day my former colleague sell it back to me, if the chance arose.

As soon as the decision to move to Norway was made, Kate perked up. She seemed happier, more engaged. I realized that her emotional batteries had gotten really low. My own were not exactly supercharged. I tried to look on the bright side. Maybe this move was the best thing for us? After all, they say that a change is as good as a rest.

On one level, I was excited about moving to a new country. I love travel and challenges and new places. But there was a heavy shadow hanging over me and I was nothing less than devastated to be leaving Delphinus behind.

But at least it was not going anywhere. Even if I did not use her for a while, I would come back to her, I was sure. We did our best to leave the boat as spic and span as possible. We emptied the water tank, and winterized the engine and I left little packets of desiccants in the lockers to absorb moisture.

Already in my mind I was planning the following year's vacation. We could return in the summer months and really dedicate some time to sailing, I believed.

Perhaps it was possible to combine our dreams? Kate wanted traditional stability, and I needed the freedom that the boat gave me. Could we find a compromise that made us both happy?

It was mid-April when we finally moved to Oslo. There was still snow on the ground and it was cold. This was not my first visit to the country, having been there regularly during my college years. But this was not a flying visit during Easter break; this was permanent relocation.

As always, money, or rather, its lack, was an issue. I needed to get a job immediately, so I started to write job applications and sending out my CV. Amazingly, I got a lot of interest and quickly found a well-paying job that required my attendance between 9-5.

After six weeks, we found a house we could afford, and I got a loan from the bank. The grey of winter was fading, the snows were melting and spring was definitely in the air. The novelty of my new country had not waned and I should have been excited about the future, but all I could think about was what we had left standing in a corner of the marina under the oak tree.

We now had neighbors who seemed incredibly near. I knew when they were up, since I could smell their cigarette smoke and I could hear their muffled voices through the walls. Even when they were not fighting with each other.

We had a nice enough house, but we had lost the biggest yard imaginable. We used to have the whole outdoors. Now we had a patch of scrubby grass with what looked like the neighbor's dog's poop on it.

I had expected things to improve between Kate and myself. But now that we were back to four walls and a picket fence, things did not really get any better. Those moods that I had thought were the result of being cramped aboard a small boat did not diminish. If anything, they worsened. The entire premise of our moving to Norway was to make Kate's life easier and to be closer to her family. But if Kate had felt isolated on the boat, she appeared to be just as isolated now.

Her family were far from the helpful, caring troupe that she had described. Not once did anyone offer to babysit so we could have a night out together. And although we saw them from time to time, at best, all that one could say is that now they lived relatively close by.

We were both disappointed, and this did not help our relationship. Kate was angry at her family for failing to make good on their promise, and she was angry at me for pointing it out. It seemed that there was a lot of anger going around in those days.

In the end, Kate chose to end our marriage and I did not contest it. Almost immediately, I felt a huge weight lift from my shoulders. I had never really understood just how much I had been carrying until that moment.

Far from being unhappy about the situation, I realized that this could be an opportunity. After all, I had wanted freedom and now it looked like Kate was giving it to me. Here was my chance to live whatever life I wanted. Delphinus was exactly where we had left it. All I had to do was pack a bag and I could pick up where I had left off.

I moved out of my home and took a room in a shared house. I had a bed, my clothes and a computer. It was not much to hold me down. But at least I had a job.

My old buddy Steve had been in a similar pickle after his divorce and he had started again. He had moved across the country and created a new life for himself. I was on the wrong side of the Atlantic for the life that I wanted, but I knew that it would not be difficult to buy a plane ticket and go back to Annapolis.

The question of what I would do next was never far from my mind but I had something that Steve did not; my children.

It was at that time that things began to take a serious downturn for me. That well-paid job I had landed when I first arrived in Norway suddenly dried up and I was downsized. Now I was a jobless, penniless and probably soon homeless immigrant. I could feel my options closing by the minute.

The room I had rented overlooked the Oslo fjord. While the view was spectacular, especially during sunset, it was in an old house without insulation and by winter it got very cold. This felt like a fitting season for the current phase of my life. I shared the house with a couple of other recent relationship rejects, which is a lot less fun that it sounds.

Now that I did not have a job and was almost out of money, things could not be much worse. I was newly separated and desperately lonely. I saw my kids every other week, which was time I cherished. But I was living in a country where I had no friends or family and could not even speak the language.

My dream of living the good life was over. Now I was doing my best just to survive.

Chapter 15 – Lemons and Mangoes

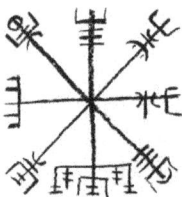

"A table, a chair, a bowl of fruit and a violin; what else
does a man need to be happy?"
~ *Albert Einstein*

Life had well and truly delivered a pile of lemons to
my door. But, as an eternal optimist, my natural
instinct was to toss them out and get some mangoes.
What do I mean by that? Well, simply put, I wanted to
change the playing field, change the rules.

That sounds easy, but exactly how do you do that?
After all, I was living in a country that did not need me
and where I could not see a future. Not such an easy
thing to change, in spite of my desperation.

I wanted to stay in Norway so that I could continue
to be an influence on my kids' lives, but with no
means to support myself, no savings, and only a tiny
room in a shared house to call my own, I was not in a
position to do very much for myself, let alone for
them.

Einstein once said that all a man needed to be
happy was a table, a chair, a bowl of fruit and a violin.
Let me tell you something. He was wrong. I needed
more. I needed freedom and I wanted someone to
share it with. If you have that, *and* a bowl of fruit and
a violin then you are doing okay!

At the back of my mind was the knowledge that all I had to do was book a flight and I could continue my dream, albeit alone. This was what everyone expected me to do. It was the obvious decision, and on more than one occasion, people asked when I would be going back to the US.

At that point, I felt as if I had no real choice. The alternative was an almost insurmountable challenge. I would have to learn a foreign language from scratch, find another job in a market where the bubble had well and truly burst and then buy a house, all without friends, family or money to help lighten the load.

Of course, I considered the alternative. Going back to the US, would be easy. I already had a place to live, since Delphinus had been moved ashore and was simply waiting to go back into the water. Plus, I was certain that I could find another job somewhere, with my experience and qualifications. And finally, I had friends there. Yet, as tempting and easy as it would have been, I could not do it. The idea of my kids growing up without me was a pill too bitter to swallow.

I am sure my own childhood had much to do with my decision. My own father had left when I was a small child, barely five years old. I have very few memories of him. Either he was not around much or time has erased him from my mind. In fact, perhaps the only incident that I can recall with any clarity was a time we went to a park.

Interlude 1969

The picnic was a mess of crumbs and paper plates and half eaten peanut butter and jelly sandwiches. Nearby, a kid with a pudding bowl haircut laughed and chased the Frisbee that his father tossed. The kid's brother grabbed it up from the ground where it rolled to a stop and threw it back to their father. Like the piggy in the middle, the younger boy chased it frantically, laughing.

After a while, tired of the game, the young boy wandered off to the edge of the park where a group of kids and their fathers were sailing wooden boats with little sails. He stared at them in wonder then ran back and grabbed his father's hand, dragging him to the pond.

"Daddy, can we do that?" He pointed at the little boats that were gently bobbing up and down, hardly moving in the lighter than light breeze.

The boy's father shrugged.

"We don't have a boat."

The kid's face fell. Then inspiration hit. "Can we buy one?" He looked up hopefully, but his father's frown informed him of the answer before the crushing words came.

"No, we can't."

The kid did not sigh or pout, but he turned away disappointed. Then his father spoke again.

"But maybe we can make one."

The boy was puzzled. He looked at the sleek craft on the water with their little sails and lines. Make a boat?

His father strode back to the picnic where the kid's mother was reading a newspaper. He extracted a section of the paper, then knelt on the blanket, folding and creasing a page. In a moment he was done, and he walked back to the pond, a little paper boat cradled in his hands.

"Here. Put this in the water and give it a push."

The boy smiled, delighted. This was better than anything the other kids had! His father handed him a stick, and the kid pushed the boat, carefully balancing on the pond's edge. The boat did not last long. It soaked up water and was soon a soggy mess. The kid fished it out with his stick where it limply hung.

"Don't worry," his father said. "We can make another."

* * *

That was perhaps the only positive memory from my childhood of my father. He left us soon after that and started another family. I imagine that a therapist would read something into this. But whatever suppressed trauma I might have there was a question that I grappled with. Could I do this to my own kids? For perhaps the first time in my life, I was overwhelmed. I felt that I was drowning and I simply did not know what I could do.

Then, one day, a serendipitous discovery spurred me into making a life changing decision.

In 1969, Kris Kristofferson wrote the immortal line, 'Freedom's just another word for nothing left to lose.' You probably recognize it from the song, '*Me and Bobby McGee.*' It is a plaintive and bitter sweet lament about regret, and has long been a favorite of mine.

I remember first hearing this song as a child. I liked the melody, but I never thought about the meaning of the lyrics. But one afternoon, the song came on the radio and it happened: I had an epiphany. I realized that the aforementioned Bobby was a woman!

I felt like someone had played a grand trick on me. For a moment I was outraged, then amused. I was probably not the only one who did not know Bobby McGee was a lady. There are probably millions of people who thought, as I did, that Bobby was a man. And if so many people can be so wrong about that, then maybe everyone was wrong about me!

From that moment I was confirmed in my decision. I would show them. All those who assumed that I would take the easy road and return to the US were wrong. I was not going to give up. I would fight!

I set about creating a plan of action. First, I needed my own place. A rental that I could afford, but one that would give me enough extra space for the kids to stay over. Then I would focus on learning the language. That was critical to my finding a job, then I could eventually buy a house.

And that was my plan. It was simple, but the goals were concrete and attainable.

The 'trick' to achieving any goal is to have a clear idea of what you want, and make a plan that will, by hook or by crook, get you there.

This may not always be easy and there will be unexpected road blocks that will bar your way, forcing you into any number of detours. After all, no battle plan survives contact with the enemy.

There were a lot of variables to consider (such as where I was going to get the money from to pay the three months deposit for an apartment) but I had made a decision and that is what mattered.

I poured myself a drink and held it up in a silent toast to myself, the Gods of fate and to Norway.

I would have to give up my dream of cruising on the world's oceans, at least for now. It was a sad thought, but I had something more important than my own needs to consider. I was determined not to abandon my children the way my father had abandoned me.

Perhaps I felt a bit sorry for myself? My own childhood had not always been easy and I did not want my own kids to experience what I had. So a little self-righteous pity may have inspired me to imbibe a little more grog than usual.

I had never been much of a drinker, but I got three sheets to the wind that day. In truth, it is rare thing for me to be drunk (ever since an incident celebrating Queen Elizabeth's Silver Jubilee in 1977) but I felt as if I were at a wake. After all, my dream had just died; it should be commemorated.

Three sheets to the wind is such an odd expression and I cannot help but chuckle when I hear it. In case you are not familiar with it, 'three sheets' is a metaphor for someone drinking too much. It comes from England's naval heritage, as do many colorful expressions. However, it is not quite correct. The original phrase was actually "three sheets *in* the wind."

This might seem like a minor distinction, but when you stop to consider what the phrase is actually saying, it makes perfect sense. The 'sheets' aren't sails, as most people think, but the ropes tied to the sails to hold them in place. If three sheets are loose and blowing about in the wind then the sail will flap about like a drunken sailor, hence the expression.

I have to admit, I really like maritime expressions, although they do not make up for me becoming a landlubber. And yes, there's another!

So, now that I was determined to remain in Norway, I needed to find a way to dispose of all those lemons that had been piling up at my door.

I would need money and I had only one asset of any value that I could easily liquidate. It was not an easy decision and there is almost never a day that I do not regret it, but Delphinus was the only thing that could keep my head above water.

Fran took care of the sale. It seemed only fitting that she should do it, since she already knew the boat, and knew what we had done with it.

Once the money was wired to me, I transferred half to Kate. What I was left with was modest, to say the least. If I was careful, it would keep me going for three months.

While this was going on, I tried my best to force load a new language into my brain. It was slow going, but my Norwegian ability improved and I quickly learned enough to be capable of embarrassing myself in almost any situation.

Since I was not working, I tried to keep busy with exercise. Running, circuit training, etc. I lost weight and my fitness improved. I slowly started to come to terms with losing my family, while the kids and I got used to the routine of visits every other weekend. But the biggest thing that I did was send off hundreds and hundreds of job applications.

When I had first arrived in the country, IT jobs were ten a penny. But now it seemed that they were bitterly contested. I was up against people who were as qualified as I was *and* could speak the language natively. My chances were severely hampered as a result.

I wrote applications for jobs that I was wildly unqualified for, but beggars, as they say, cannot be choosers. I would apply for anything that would pay a steady wage and enable me to establish myself in a country that seemed determined to spit me out.

While I was an undergrad student in the United Kingdom, I had worked in a hotel washing dishes as well as in a retirement home for the elderly. I did not particularly love either job but experience had taught me that there is always work that someone does not want and if you are desperate you can find it. Well, I was desperate, and I was willing to wash dishes and change adult diapers if I had to.

It took a while, but in the end, that was not

necessary. One of my applications met with interest, and I was invited to an interview.

It was for an institute that did environmental research. This sounded good to me. After all, if I had to work in an office, then let it be for something worthwhile. Plus, I had always had an interest in Nature and the world around me, so environmental research seemed like a golden opportunity.

I got the job.

From that point, my life seemed to turn around and things improved. I bought a motorcycle, importing it from England. I also started to date, and after some hit and misses, met someone I really liked, a young lady named Alisa.

It had taken me a couple of years of real struggle, but by then I could honestly say that I was back on my feet.

I had a good job, I could speak Norwegian passably well and I began to regard the cold North as my home. I still thought about Delphinus and what I had left behind, but that was another life in another world.

Things with Alisa quickly became serious and the following year we were married. A new chapter in my life had begun, and as much as I might wish for it, there was no boat in my future. I had commitments and I was damn well going to live up to them.

Thanks to Fred Foster and Kris Kristofferson I had stuck it out in Norway. Little did I know that this was going to be my home for the best part of the next two decades.

Chapter 16 – Another Picket Fence

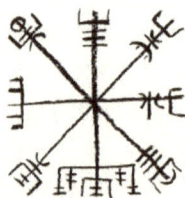

"It's the spirit within, not the veneer without, that makes a man."

~ *Sir Robert Baden-Powell*

Interlude, 2014

The hall was full to bursting. Rows of closely packed chairs were occupied by the parents, siblings and grandparents of the two dozen members of the scout troupe who milled about in happy confusion. Unlike the original boy scout's organization, in Norway it is a mixed group with boys and girls taking part in activities and trips together.

Excited youngsters raced around, ignoring their parents who tried vainly to control them. I settled myself into a chair by a wall and waited for the show to begin.

The program for the night included aspirants being inducted into the troupe, as well as a host of kids getting badges and awards. There also some music and 'skits' where the troupe members acted out amusing incidents from their trips, or performed song and dance routines for us.

My girls had both joined the Scouts at a relatively young age and had been active members for years. Tonight would see my eldest daughter receive the

'Speidersjefens topputmerkelse,' which I translate as 'Scout Chief's Top Award.'

It was a nice evening, and I had fun watching my girls do their thing, including a hilarious dance routine that had the audience in stitches. Whenever there were announcements or speeches, I did not really understand everything. In the noisy crowd, the words were too fast and indistinct for me to grasp.

I am not very well integrated into Norwegian society, although I am happy to say that my kids are. They are a perfect illustration of second-generation immigrants. They are fluent in both Norwegian and English, and thanks to the Scouts, enjoy typical Norwegian activities, such as skiing, hiking, sleeping in snow holes, and generally messing around in the woods and mountains.

These are not areas in which I have any experience. We did not have a scout group in the area where I grew up. The scouts taught them things I could not, and I am grateful for that. And even though I had hoped to give my girls a life on the water, I was happy to see that they were highly adept and capable in both the forest and the mountains.

Still, I wish that I could have done more with them, such as taking them to places where they could learn about marine life and how important the oceans are to our continued existence. Deep inside, I still harbored a dream that it would happen. In fact, when I slept, I sometimes felt the rocking motion of the boat, only to be disappointed when I awoke.

However, my life took a different course. Now I was firmly tied down. The kids, my work, my house, all ensured that I would stay put for many a year to come.

The oceans would have to wait.

* * *

This was the pact I made with myself in order to be able to support my girls. Being a father is a duty and as much joy as I felt in the role, there was certainly a price.

I had entered into an era of living to work, instead of working to live. It was a mistake, and I knew it.

Life became routine and I looked forward to my weekends and vacations as much as any other working stiff. Yet I never once forgot what I had given up and I continued to dream about the time that I would buy another boat and pursue that endless sunset. Like Dan from South Bend, I figured that I would have to do my time, retire, and then maybe have a shot at finally living the 'good life.'

If you have not come across the short story by Heinrich Böll, about a fisherman who does just enough to live his dream, then I urge you to check it out. Written in 1963, and called "Anekdote zur Senkung der Arbeitsmoral" or "Anecdote on the lowering of work moral" (my own translation) it is a short story, much like a Biblical parable and tells the story of a businessman on vacation in a small fishing village somewhere in Europe.

The businessman tries to encourage a fisherman to work hard, grow his business and become a huge success so that he may finally sell his business empire and reap the rewards of his efforts. And what is that reward? Why, to retire to a small fishing village, where he can relax, enjoy his family, take siestas and enjoy the good life, etc.

Naturally, the fisherman points out that he is already doing just that . . . He already has plenty of time to relax, enjoy his family and take siestas, etc. And he does not have to work very long or hard to achieve it.

Aside from the fact that the story is amazingly

succinct, it is both amusing and full of pathos. The businessman sees an opportunity to achieve the good life through decades of hard work, while the fisherman is already living the good life. He has all he needs to be happy already. He probably has a bowl of fruit and a violin too.

The main point of the story, as I see it, is why work your whole life to achieve an objective that is already within your grasp? Or, to put it another way, why waste your life attempting to attain a lifestyle that you can enjoy right now?

I love that story and consider it as almost a template for how a person can live the dream, without first having to sacrifice their whole life to achieve it. The secret, I believe, is to have *modest ambitions*.

If you want to live in expensive hotels and have people wait on you, then probably you need to follow the businessman's advice. But if you are interested in a life not defined by materialism, if you are frugal and self-reliant, then I believe that a simpler approach may work.

I have modest ambitions. I am not interested in expensive watches or high-priced sneakers. I don't care too much about what car I drive or eating out in fancy restaurants.

None of that matters to me. What I want is to work for myself. I want to get up when I feel like it, not when the alarm demands. I want to have a relaxed morning and eat breakfast with my family, then catch up on world events. I want to write what I want, when I want. I would like to be healthy, happy and satisfied.

These, it seems to me, are not only modest ambitions, but some of them (to be healthy and happy, for example) should be a basic human right.

Okay, to be fair, I would like to do all these things on a boat in the Bahamas, but I do not insist on it!

However, when it comes to the reason why I have not managed to achieve my ambitions, modest or otherwise, I am forced to face an unpleasant and rather inconvenient truth. It is because I chose not to.

Why do I make decisions that I know do not make me happy? Why do I allow myself to be put into a position where I cannot even achieve the most modest of my ambitions, that of having breakfast with my family?

I can sum up my problem in one word; work. Like everyone else, I have to work long hours in order to earn the money we need to maintain the house and cars, and buy clothes and food and so on. But after thirty-five years of working hard, I would have thought that it was enough. That finally, I could be who I wanted and do what I wanted. Yet a quick glance at my bank account informs me that this is, as always, impossible.

Aside from a brief period in my twenties, before I knew enough to know that I knew nothing, I have been a wage slave. Every paycheck and every penny I have earned has gone to supporting my family and all the trappings of modern life.

And even as I write this, I am thinking that there are millions who would like to be in my shoes. Maybe even billions! How can I be so selfish? How can I complain about having to work hard, so long as I see that my family are well fed and we have a nice house, and we live a comfortable life?

The fact is, I am wracked with guilt. I should be happy that we are doing okay financially, since many are not. I should be happy that my family is healthy, even if I am not. And yet, there is a part of my conscience that nags me. Like a tiny devil on my shoulder, whispering into my ear.

"You did your duty for longer than should be

necessary. Now what about you?"

Am I even allowed to think like that? And, even more crazy, am I allowed to expect that my life can be lived in accordance with my own wishes?

Yes, I say. Yes!

And yet, I resist. Almost a lifetime of indoctrination has made me believe that everyone's needs are more important than my own. I don't need to tell you that this is both a depressing situation as well as something of a revelation.

Ever since I was a kid, I have been a rebel. Like Groucho, I would not want to belong to any club that would have me and I avoided any teenage trend that became part of the zeitgeist.

All I knew was that I did not want to be part of the establishment. But now I was so entrenched with my job and mortgage and credit card debt that I *was* the establishment.

"What are you rebelling against, kid?"

"Whadda you got?"

If I was going to rebel, it would have to be against my own nature. Even though Delphinus was gone, I knew that I could get another boat. Something better, something bigger! Once again I became consumed with 'the dream.' But first, I had to convince Alisa that giving up her walk-in closet was a good thing and that we did not really need jobs or money to be happy. It was not going to be easy. She *really* liked that closet.

Chapter 17 – Second Bite of the Cherry

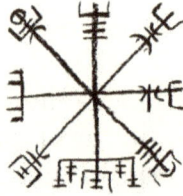

"He went like one that hath been stunned,
And is of sense forlorn:
A sadder and a wiser man,
He rose the morrow morn."
~ *Samuel Taylor Coleridge*

All relationships have problems. As the years passed and my children grew and I got older and fatter, my relationship with Alisa went through a series of highs and lows.

We took a vacation to Key West, which was a dream destination for us both. For Alisa, it was all about warm water and sunshine and white sandy beaches, while for me, I mostly wanted to walk the docks and look at boats or stare out to the horizon and wonder what was beyond.

We had a great time, with walking the sunny streets and snorkeling at the Dry Tortugas (dry turtles?) but that is not to say that we did not have issues. Our relationship had hit a low point, and it was not easily overcome simply by going on vacation, even in a place as magical as the Florida Keys.

Key West really is incredible. It is an island that lies at the tip of an archipelago of about 1700 islands.

They begin at the southeastern tip of the Florida peninsula, about 15 miles or 24 kilometers south of Miami, and extend in an arc to Key West, and the uninhabited Tortugas.

Key West is actually closer to Cuba than it is to Miami, so you get an idea that it is likely to be a warm, tropical island. And it is.

Of course, that is only one aspect of the island's character. It has many; a long history, plenty of events year-round, and a wealth of charming old houses and colonial architecture to mention a few more.

It also has some rather more unusual attributes. For instance, you cannot cross the street without several chickens following you. No, this is not a "why did the chicken cross the road" joke. These are the famous 'gypsy chickens.'

Chickens were a part of everyday life in Key West. They were a source of food, eggs, and sadly they were the ill-fated recruits for the now illegal practice of cock fighting.

When the practice was outlawed, the chicken population increased and in their endless quest for food they began to spread across the island. I found them a constant source of amusement.

Something else that everyone who visits soon learns, is that Key West is closely connected to two American icons, Ernest Hemingway and Tennessee Williams.

Hemingway wrote 'A Farewell to Arms' and Williams wrote 'A Streetcar named Desire' while resident on the island. Both are part of the American literary canon. Hemingway in particular is identified with Key West and you can still get a beer in his favorite bar and eat swordfish in his favorite restaurant.

I liked the bar (Sloppy Joe's, on Duval Street) when

we visited it on a couple of occasions. It had a good crowd, live music, and it is the site of the Hemingway look-alike contest where men with bushy, white beards gather! In 2006, it was even added to the National Register of Historic Places.

Of course, if you are really a Hemingway fan, you might be interested to know that the current location for Sloppy Joe's is not the original bar that Hemingway drank in. This is a few doors down to the west, at 428 Green Street and is now called "Captain Tony's." Having said that, there is also a third claim to be the original Sloppy Joe's, but since that is in Cuba, I won't bother to go into details.

But whatever the case, where better to get your daily dose of culture than a bar that serves good beer and music?

Another thing of interest (at least to people like me) is the fact that Key West is where Pan American Airlines first began, running planes to Havana.

Key West is a fascinating and lovely island, and I could easily imagine living there. Yes, the wanderlust was upon me again. I had begun to dream of clear waters and endless sunsets, brought on, no doubt, by the clear waters and endless sunsets of the Keys.

I wanted another bite of the cherry, and I wanted Alisa to want it too. About four years into our marriage, and not long after that visit to Key West, I proposed that we buy a boat in Florida and use it as a vacation home.

I still had the dream, and I was willing to try just about anything to make it real.

My plan was to persuade Alisa to try out the boating life, showing her only its best side; the romantic sunsets, the beauty of nature, the romance of the sea, and get her well and truly hooked on the lifestyle before broaching anything as insane as actually living in a boat.

I thought that, in time, she would come to love it as much as I did and that she would give up her walk-in closet and *share* the dream.

Although somewhat dubious, Alisa agreed to a series of stringent cutbacks so that we could save money like never before. Then I got her to agree that we would sell our house and buy a tiny little one-room apartment. This was a critical part of my deviously cunning plan, although, in retrospect, it may have been what almost destroyed our marriage.

In our new apartment, space was at a premium, so it was vital to only keep what we really needed. Again, I went through the process of eliminating a lot of things that had no place in the future that I had envisioned for us.

After we sold and gave away what we could, I rented a huge dumpster and we filled it with goodness knows what, but filled it was. With the house now empty, we sold it and moved into our new place with a good deal more money and a good deal less stuff.

Our bed was a convertible couch. A small dining room table and two chairs and some shelves were practically all the furniture we had. There was no fruit bowl or violin, but we did not miss them!

If you have ever lived in a boat, this probably sounds about right with regards to the furniture. But having moved from a four-bedroom house, with more space than we knew what to do with, it was a major shock to the system. Even with my own experience as a liveaboard, I struggled to adjust initially to our new tiny home. At only 22 square meters, or about 236 square feet, it could barely qualify as a home at all.

But nothing good is gained without effort. I wanted that sunset, and all the problems that owning and living in a boat engendered, and I was willing to do anything to achieve it, even if it meant selling all my guitars and the music gear that I had collected in the last five years. In the end, I had one guitar left. I consoled myself with the knowledge that one is all you need.

Liquidating assets can be a messy and painful experience, but so was living in a cupboard. Our tiny new home was smaller than some bathrooms!

Since Alisa had agreed to the idea of buying a boat and going to Florida during our vacations to sail it, I became dedicated to only one thing; getting a vessel that would suit our needs.

I researched, I trawled the online databases and I was patient. I was not just looking for a good, solid liveaboard, but it had to be 'turnkey.' Preferably with a lot of recent investments that the current owner had no chance of seeing a return on.

I focused on boats made in the 70s. Sure, they are old, but if I had learned one thing from Delphinus, it is that boats of that era are solid. All it would need would be a refit. And if it so happened that the previous owner had performed this solid service and then was willing to sell the boat for a song, then I would be quite open to buying it.

There were a couple motor sailors and a few trawlers that caught my eye, but none more than a Schucker 44.

I joined several forums and started talking to owners of these rare boats. It was then that I was contacted by a yacht broker. He offered to be my 'man on the ground' and keep an eye out for a bargain.

I sent him a long email, where I made clear what I was looking for in my new boat. I summarized with the following list:

1) Comfortable liveaboard. This is more important than offshore capabilities.

2) Full Displacement preferred

3) Beamy

4) Prefer single screw

5) Cruise at 6-8 knots

6) Single stateroom is fine

7) Single head is preferred (sizeable holding would be good)

8) Full size shower (the kind where you can actually stand without having to suck your gut in...)

9) Should be at least 36' length, up to maybe 44'.

The very first point I made was a direct response to having lived in a small sailboat. Size matters, don't kid yourself.

I was more realistic this time, more experienced. After two years living in a small sailboat as a family of four, I knew that we had to get a boat that served its primary purpose well. It *had* to be comfortable to live aboard.

My new broker was instrumental in finding the right boat. We communicated via email, and sent many missives back and forth across the Atlantic.

Eventually he negotiated for the purchase of a Schucker 44. It was located somewhere on the Steinhatchee River in Florida.

The boat had undergone a series of recent upgrades, which included bottom peeling, new Northern Lights GenSet, 2 A/C systems, extra fuel tank, new depth sounder, a shiny new Raymarine Chart plotter and depth Sounder, new dripless shaft seal and more. Plus, there was a very recent (two-month-old) survey, so we had a good idea of the condition.

The last owner had spent an additional $30K on

the upgrades after purchasing the boat, and he was willing to take a beating on the price. To suggest that he was motivated to sell was an understatement. Naturally, I was a little suspicious as to why he would want out so soon after he had gotten in. I asked my broker about it.

It seems that he had been a little impulsive with buying the Schucker. He had no experience with a boat that large, and had insisted on sailing it from Sarasota to Alabama with two friends that had even less experience on the water (this sounds like something I would do). When they went offshore, they experienced 6-8-foot waves and quickly became seasick and scared. Because they were too weak to operate the boat they headed to shore, finally leaving the boat on the Steinhatchee River.

Several months passed, and the owner appeared to have no desire to return for his boat. This was exactly the opportunity that I had hoped for.

We made the deal and arranged for a delivery captain to bring it down to Sarasota. I made arrangements for the boat to be stored, transferred the funds to the broker, and before long my new boat was on its way to the Manatee River and Snead Island Boat Works.

I flew to the US and sealed the deal, inspecting the boat personally for the first time. She was a beauty. She was big, built like a tank and was an unimaginably better liveaboard than Delphinus.

I was back in business! All I had to do was convince Alisa that a life of adventure and travel and drinks with little umbrellas in them was waiting. I did not feel bad about my slightly deceptive method of persuading Alisa about the virtues of sailing, since I was fully prepared to deliver on my promise of an exotic, white sand, blue sky lifestyle.

So, with the first part of my plan complete, I moved the boat ashore, went home and extolled its virtues the way a first-time parent does their newborn.

We made plans to visit the boat together. This occurred in the Easter period which pretty much guaranteed that the weather would be good, a key requirement when convincing someone of the benefits of life afloat.

Meanwhile, I requested the marina to ensure that the batteries were charged. Then I asked them to put the boat in the water and find a slip for her.

I had decided to call our new home, Hyperion. This is a good name for a boat, in my opinion. Hyperion was one of the children of Gaia and Uranus. He was a Titan and the father of Helios. At no point did I consider Delphinus II as a name choice. It seemed disrespectful.

Hyperion was put in a transit slip for a week, while Alisa and I took possession. It was a strange thing to go aboard a boat and marvel at the size, but my cunning plan had, to a surprising degree, worked well.

After our tiny apartment, the boat felt huge. There were rooms! Separate rooms, with beds, and a bathroom, and a stove, and tables, and so much more than we had at home. Well, maybe I exaggerate slightly. To be fair, we did have a toilet and a shower in our apartment. But the boat may well have had more actual living space. It sure felt that way.

Our first days on board were good and we could easily imagine living aboard. It had more closet space than our apartment! What else could anyone ask for?

Also, The Manatee River was aptly named, as we frequently saw one of the gentle beasts nosing about our stern. I am not sure what it was looking for, since they eat vegetation and our hull was clean as a whistle, but it was there at least once a day.

The fact that we had so much sunshine (remember, we had just flown in from Norway, where sunshine is restricted to roughly one hour per year) and the water was clear and abundantly full of sea life, ensured that we were both enchanted with the experience.

Watching the manatee nosing around the boat was extraordinary. And we had not even left the dock! Not to mention the pelican that insisted our coachroof was its home. Imagine what we would discover when we finally got cruising and exploring the Gulf of Mexico? I could not wait to find out.

We only spent a week on the boat, and we never took her out on the Gulf. There was an issue with the engine, that, while not particularly serious, required a mechanic, and we simply could not schedule one during our time there. We were relegated to a dockside condo for the duration of our trip.

This was not the worst thing in the world. Alisa liked the boat, which was all that mattered, and we achieved some of the objectives I had set out for us, including enjoying a drink at sunset, albeit sans little umbrellas. There was no question in my mind that it would be a very good cruising vessel. I was optimistic about the future.

However, in retrospect, I realize that I made a serious error in judgement in how I approached my reluctant spouse. Instead of enticing Alisa with promises of sunsets and margaritas, I should have attempted to engage her in a more pragmatic manner, such as ensuring that she was responsible for the boat, and its systems as much as I was.

Instead of merely being a pampered passenger, it would have been better to ensure that Alisa was part of the boat buying process. From boat selection to negotiation and finally to inspecting the boat with a critical eye, in much the same way that we had tackled buying a new apartment together.

Giving Alisa the opportunity to be both creative, and to have a say in the buying process would have engaged her and sparked a sense of ownership. As it was, the boat was my baby, my dream, and Alisa was just there for the ride with no emotional investment.

This was a huge mistake.

At the time, I did not consider this at all. I was just so hell bent on getting back to the water that I did not really care about anything else.

Alisa did enjoy adding some personal touches to Hyperion, such as choosing bedding and the usual array of things one needs to live aboard, but she had missed the essential process that would have helped her to feel it was as much her *home* as it was a boat.

Nevertheless, in spite of the fact that we could not take Hyperion out and put her to her paces, I considered that our trip had been a success. When we got back to Norway, we began to make plans for the summer where we would spend a full month cruising.

After all those years in the wilderness of Norway, I was finally going to realize the dream. The future seemed golden. I visualized years of sailing and exploring, and while it would be expensive to fly between Norway and the US, it would be worth it. Perhaps in time we could extend our stays on the boat from one month, to two, to three?

The future did indeed carry a promise. But it was not to be. Those storm clouds over our relationship that had first shown themselves in Key West had not dissipated and the new boat did not help. Frankly, the whole process probably exacerbated our issues. And things between myself and Alisa became worse than ever.

I did not know it at the time, but after that first, bitter sweet visit, I would never see Hyperion again.

Chapter 18 – A Hiccup

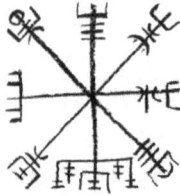

"Out of life's school of war: What does not destroy me, makes me stronger."

~ *Friedrich Nietzsche*

There is no point in sugar coating it. Alisa and I were having trouble and neither of us were happy. We argued a lot, she would cry and refuse to talk to me and I would get angry. I wanted to confront things head on, but our different approaches to handling problems only seemed to strengthen the divide.

In spite of my feelings on the matter, we agreed to separate. Not a tentative, 'try it out and see how it feels' kind of separation, but a full-on revocation of all marital duties, obligations and considerations.

For the second time in six years, I was given an opportunity to go my own way. Faced with the question of continuing my life in Norway, or moving back to the US and rebuilding my life on my own terms, I went through the same process as I had previously. But I was not even tempted. I simply could not justify moving away from my girls. Not to mention the fact that I was still very much in love with Alisa, and I secretly harbored the idea that we would reconcile one day.

She did not know how I felt, and I did not tell her. I hoped that, in time, she would conclude that breaking up was a mistake and that what she really needed in her life was me. I was patient, I could wait. I had been in this position before, when I was much younger and less sure of myself. That did not work out as I had hoped, but I was certain that this time it would be different.

For the next several months, we both did our own thing. In truth, although we lived apart and in spite of what we had agreed, we had not truly separated. And even though Alisa now had a boyfriend and I had a girlfriend, somehow we found ourselves spending more and more of our time together.

Any fool could see that we were not willing to let each other go, but Alisa had to work something out of her system and I was willing to wait while she did.

Eventually, my faith was rewarded. In less than six months, our separation ended.

It happened after we had been out to dinner together. She looked at me coyly as we drove back to my apartment. I noticed, but did not say anything. She seemed to have something on her mind. After so many years, I knew not to press. It would come in its own time.

In one of the best days of my life, Alisa informed me that if I would take her back, she would like to continue to be my wife. I informed her that nothing would make me happier. She moved in with me, and we became a couple again.

For weeks, I could not stop grinning. We were back!

I had already bought another apartment, which was considerably bigger than the 22 square meter cupboard we had shared together when I was hell bent on acclimating us to life in a small space, so we rented out the tiny apartment and made plans to buy a house, somewhere in the countryside. But nowhere in the discussions of our joint future did I mention a sailboat, in spite of the fact that it was never far from my mind. I would have to come to terms with the fact that some things are never meant to happen.

I chose my marriage over my dream. And you know what? I was happy. I thought that it was the right choice.

If we had reconciled earlier, there is a chance that we would still own Hyperion and possibly follow my original plan of vacation trips in the Gulf of Mexico. But the fact is, once we had split up, money was critical. Buying an apartment is not easy, especially when you need to find a down payment and you have only one asset worth a damn.

Amazingly, I did not actually lose money when selling Hyperion. It is a testimony to the value that an older vessel like that can have, when, even in an economy suffering a severe down turn, our 70s Schucker sold for more than we paid for it.

This is practically impossible, and it may be the first time in the annals of boating history that a boat sold for more than it was bought for. And yet we did it. It certainly meant that I had originally made a savvy choice when buying it. However, my long-cherished dream was once again coming to an end, before it even had a chance to slip its moorings.

As much as I hated it, I had to face facts. I was destined to be a landlubber for the rest of my life. This seemed even more likely now. Six months after we had become a couple again, Alisa informed me that she was pregnant.

The sea life would have to wait. We were having a baby!

Chapter 19 – A New Beginning

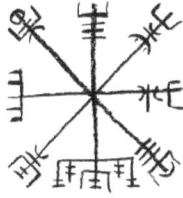

"Money often costs too much."
~ *Ralph Waldo Emerson*

The years pass swiftly when you have a youngster in tow. It is wonderful experience to watch them growing up and becoming a person with their own personality, with their own likes and dislikes. You find yourself measuring time by their birthdays and their events, such as when they first stand, or walk. And now, four years later, we were preparing for Christmas and the joy it would bring. It was full on winter and a deep chill had settled on the land, but we were snug and cozy in our old wooden house.

Outside the frosted windows, the snow blanketed the ground and trees, muffling the world and transforming the countryside into a white, crystalline wonderland.

The snow had come early. Winter, it seemed, loved Norway and wouldn't let it be. Our neighbor, a spritely eighty-year-old man, informed us that it could mean a good summer. One always hoped, but never too hard. It did not do to have high expectations of the Sun this far north of the equator.

I put another log on the fire, then used a thick splinter of wood to poke its red heart until it roared.

Alisa was curled up on the sofa, entranced by her book. Our daughter, Riley, sat on the rug, staring up at the wall-mounted television, tittering at the antics of a cartoon bear.

Family life had caught up with me again. But far from railing against it, I was generally content. Perhaps the near miss that Alisa and I had undergone had 'scared me straight?' I don't know, but whatever the case, I was writing, working, and being a father, all things that I love and I was not interested in changing anything.

Of course, I had not forgotten my dream. I had simply put it away, high up on a shelf where no one else could see it. I had accepted another in its place; a dream with white picket fences and kid's parties and mowing the lawn on Sunday afternoons. Of course, that was really Alisa's dream, but I adopted it as my own and for a good while I was happy.

At that moment, Alisa looked up and stared out of the window at the snow driving against the glass. She frowned slightly and lowered her book. Not overly fond of the cold, or snow, unsurprisingly her thoughts were on warmer climes.

"What should we do in the summer?"

"Vacation you mean?" I replied.

"Yes."

"No idea," I added helpfully. I usually left this sort of thing to Alisa since she enjoyed browsing for hotels and vacation destinations. But in my mind, I saw sailboats and a deep blue sea. I quickly suppressed the image. "You want to go south, somewhere warm, or stay in Norway?"

"South," came her firm reply.

Living in Norway meant that we had short summers. Many were notable only for their lack of sunshine. Taking a vacation in the south of Europe had become a tradition for Norwegians in recent decades, although I say it goes back more than a thousand years. If you want to know the real reason for the Viking expansion, it was because they were all fed up with the rain and snow. This is not, I hasten to add, a theory endorsed by academics, but they don't live here so what do they know?

"We could go visit my father." I suggested. Even though he had left my family when I was six, never to return, I had gotten in contact with him again. He had retired to Costa Rica, and we had visited him there once, before Riley was born. Costa Rica is an interesting country full of warm and engaging people and I longed to return. And bonus, the weather was practically guaranteed to be good.

Alisa screwed up her face. "It's too expensive. And the flights are super long."

Yes, that was true. What with layovers, we had spent twenty-hours going just one way.

"Okay," I replied. "How about Greece."

This met with approval. All that we had to do was find a package deal that provided entertainment for kids. This was Alisa's forte, and she happily set to, searching for a suitable offer. It did not take long, and she booked a two-week trip.

Six months later and it was (allegedly) summer. But we did not care if the sun would not shine in Norway. We were on the way to a small island called Kos. It lies in the Aegean Sea, off the coast of Turkey and is part of the Dodecanese (which means, twelve islands). Aside from Kos, the only other relatively well-known island from the chain are Rhodes and Patmos.

But Kos is a lovely island, with lots of wonderful people, beaches, and plenty of wind. This last got my attention, as I could not help but wonder what it would be like to sail in such blustery conditions.

One afternoon, while we were lying on our sunbeds on the beach, I stared in envy at a sailboat in the distance.

"Nice," Alisa said as she dried her hair with a towel. I nodded. It was nice. Better than nice.

"Yeah, they're on a beam reach. Really tearing it up."

Even from the distant beach, I could see that the boat's toe rail was buried in the water.

"What's a beam reach?" Alisa enquired, shading her eyes against the sun as she watched the boat.

"That's when the wind comes from the side," I replied. "It's not quite the fastest point of sail, but close to it."

"How come?"

I debated explaining apparent wind, lift and so on. Frankly, I did not think I could do it justice. While I understood it, in principle, to actually explain it to someone else was quite another thing. I shrugged.

But I could easily imagine myself on that boat, feeling the buffeting of the waves and the salt spray and the joy of wind in the sails and almost at once, like a sickness, the longing hit me again. Clearly I had never recovered from the 'bug' and it had overwhelmed my immune system again.

I must have appeared melancholy as I slumped back on the lounger.

"What's wrong?" Alisa asked.

"Nothing," I replied. There was no point in discussing it, as I knew well from past experience.

"Don't say 'nothing' when I can see something is bothering you."

I sighed and nodded to the sailboat, which had traveled a surprising distance already.

"What?" Alisa demanded, puzzled. "You want to go

on one of those sunset cruise things?"

"No," I replied, irritated. Then I thought about it. "Well, actually, I would love to. But that's not what's bothering me."

I decided that there was no harm in admitting the truth. The last time we had discussed the topic it had not gone too well, and I could not see that anything had changed. But since she asked.

"I want another boat."

Alisa flopped down on the sunbed next to mine. Riley ran up and showed us an interesting shell she had found. We both admired it, and she ran off to find more.

"Well, if we could sail somewhere like this, it wouldn't be too bad," Alisa said with a wave at the pristine blue of the sea.

I almost fell off the sunbed in surprise (this is pure hyperbole. In actual fact, I found it very difficult to get off the damned things).

"Really? You'd like to try your hand at sailing?"

"Well, I don't know about that. But I wouldn't mind *being* on a sailboat. Especially here."

It was a beautiful location. An ideal place to island hop and swim in warm seas and snorkel. What could be better than the Greek isles?

"How about we come back next year and rent a boat? We could potter around in the Med for a couple of weeks?"

Alisa stared out at the water. She did not say anything for moment as she considered my offer.

"Actually, that sounds great."

I grinned with excitement. Did my wife secretly harbor a desire to sail? Was she just placating me? Did I even care? I decided to probe how far Alisa's seemingly new-found enthusiasm was willing to go.

"Of course, it's super expensive to hire a boat. And

what with the flights, it will cost a lot. Why don't we just buy a boat?" I said. "We can keep it somewhere on the Aegean and use it in the summers. Croatia, maybe?"

I had in mind a reprise of the Florida plan, but Alisa shot it down immediately.

"No. The travel costs would be too high," she countered. "And we couldn't use it often enough to warrant the expense. Not a good idea."

I nodded. I could not argue with her. She was right and we both knew it. Marina costs are prohibitive anywhere in the Mediterranean. I sighed and watched as the sailboat, much like my dream, disappeared around the headland.

"Oh well, I guess that's that then," I said and waved to Riley who had put a bucket on her head and looked like she was wearing an orange Fez.

Still, it had given me a brief moment of hope. I smiled ruefully and allowed myself to wallow in self-righteous disappointment. Then Alisa dropped a bombshell.

"Isn't it better if we just bought one in Norway?"

I stopped breathing. Norway? She wants to buy a boat in Norway? Yes, why not?

Instantly I started to analyze the possibility of sailing at around sixty degrees latitude. For the record, this is about the same as the city of Homer in Alaska or the Kamchatka Peninsula in Russia.

Okay, so the weather would not be good, or at least, not good for very long, but we could have a boat, sail it on weekends and during vacations. It would be cold in the evenings, so something with a full cockpit enclosure would be good.

The Oslo fjord is not a forgiving place to sail as a novice. It is long and narrow and over 500 feet deep. There are also rocks that lurk just below the surface in some places. But they would all be marked, I was sure. Well, at least, *most* of them would be marked. It would not be like sailing in the Chesapeake, but we could afford a decent GPS now, which was a change.

We would be able to explore the islands off the Swedish coast, and sail to Denmark and the west coast of Norway. The cost of owning the boat would be offset by the savings from not going on expensive foreign vacations.

It was something to think about. And the more I did, the more convinced I became that it was a *good* idea. In fact, it was a great idea!

It was not quite my dream of sailing around the world, of being a cruising sailor, but it was something. We could have a boat, we could sail as a family, and we could have fun together. Maybe, in time, everything else would follow? After all, the longest journey begins with a single step.

I could still work, we would still live in our house, and we would only get out on the water during the all too brief summer. Longer if we got that enclosure. 'Kalosje . . .' that's what they call it, isn't it?

Not about to look a gift horse in the mouth, I immediately agreed that it sounded like a fine idea, and we should start looking into it immediately.

Later that day, I fired up my laptop and checked out what was on the used boat market in the Oslo fjord. There were plenty of suitable vessels and I felt spoiled for choice.

That trip to Kos rates as my all-time favorite vacation. I had my family, and for the first time in more years than I wanted to count, I could once again see a boat in my future.

We came home a week later and I examined our finances to figure out how we could swing a major purchase. We did not have any savings. In fact, we had a not inconsiderable mountain of debt. Should we sell the cars, the house? How much is a kidney worth?

Alisa was opposed to the idea of selling anything and resisted my automatic response to 'boat mode,' which is to get rid of everything for whatever I can and move aboard my floating home. This time I was not going to get away with it.

Autumn came, and with it a plethora of boats as owners who wished to sell vied for the few buyers willing to kick tires in winter. Within a few days, I had found some likely looking options online. Having learned something from the Florida debacle and the loss of Hyperion (which still stings) I was careful to show my choices to Alisa. She was not encouraging. Everything was too old, or not very nice, or simply did not get her excited.

"You have to consider it from other perspectives," I argued.

"Like what?"

"Seaworthiness, for one. Like, how will it perform in rough seas."

She looked me dead in the eye. "But we won't be going out in rough seas."

I nodded. One step at a time. "Sure, sure. But you never know when the wind will get up. Better to have a boat that can handle anything, right?"

Alisa looked at me suspiciously, before admitting that what I said made sense. Nevertheless, she was adamant that she was going to be a fair-weather sailor.

I was fine with that. But it was clear that I was not going to be able to dictate the choice of boat. In spite of the fact that I really wanted a Westsail 32, the most legendary and bullet proof of all cruising boats, Alisa did not like anything that appeared old fashioned. She wanted shiny and new.

We went to see an early 1980s Contessa 32. It was well used, but to me seemed like a sound enough vessel with plenty of life left in it. However, it was a little musty as most old boats are, and Alisa was put off by the strange smell. I assured her that this could be resolved with the judicious use of coffee grounds strategically placed in the head, the forepeak and the salon. They would absorb the smells in short order. Why this is so, I do not know, but it really does appear to work. I got the tip from my previous dock neighbor Steve on his Hunter. His boat was *really* musty when he got it, but he managed to tame its stinky nature.

Alisa did not care. It was more about the design, she said.

I countered with the argument that the boat was designed by David Sadler and was one of the most successful cruising and race designs.

Alisa countered with the observation that it was dark and dingy inside the salon (there was a lot of mahogany) and it reminded her of a coffin thanks to the plush purple upholstery.

Clearly, it would not do. I began to despair that nothing ever would. Our tastes were very different when it came to boats (and just about everything else, actually.

I asked Alisa to go online and show me a boat that she *did* like. She went to the local boat website and looked them over. Then she showed me a few that met with her approval. They all cost in excess of a million kroner, which is a lot of money (approximately 115,000 dollars at the time of writing) and far more than we could afford.

I have always been a budget boater. This new boat would have to be budget with a capital B.

Of course, if we had the money then I might have been interested in a luxury yacht, but that was simply not an option. However, it was clear that Alisa would only accept something new(ish).

It was going to cost us a lot more than I had anticipated. But if Alisa wanted new and shiny and most importantly, not smelly, then who was I to argue?

We increased the top purchase price and looked at more boats. Suddenly Bavaria and Beneteau were looking like options. I found one that appeared to be nothing short of a bargain; a Beneteau Clipper 311. It was everything we both wanted. A roomy coastal cruiser, easy to single-hand, clean and shiny and, best of all, 'almost' new.

Generally speaking, when you see boat pics on the Internet they only show you the best of the boat. Any horrors will be hidden, or certainly not featured. I expected this to be the case here too.

I called the owner that night and we agreed a time to meet him and view the boat.

The whole family went since we were all in this together, and there was a high degree of excitement infecting us all during the hour plus drive to the marina. Our daughter was looking forward to her first time on a pirate ship (as she insisted) and I was thrilled just to be looking at a boat.

It was a typically gray day in October and we had dressed warmly. Norwegians will tell you that there is no such thing as bad weather, only bad clothes. Like most immigrants, I took this with a pinch of salt. In my opinion there is very often bad weather!

We arrived at the marina and met Eirik, the owner of the Clipper. He had just returned from a test sail with another prospective buyer.

As we approached the slip where the boat was moored we could not see much due to a large motorboat that obscured it. But as we got closer and I finally caught sight of it all my concerns about hidden horrors seemed entirely unwarranted. It really did look as good in real life as it did in the pictures.

The Clipper 311 has a high freeboard, and this was my first indication that I had lost my edge when it came to boats. I could hardly climb aboard. My knee was simply not strong enough to lift me up. Luckily, Eirik had a fender (shaped suspiciously like a hemorrhoid cushion) which he clipped to the rail, and it made a handy step.

I vowed to begin stretching exercises as I clambered clumsily aboard. Alisa passed up our daughter then gracefully climbed aboard herself, as naturally as if she has been doing it all her life.

Riley was super excited and wanted to climb and jump from everything, but I kept firm control of her, not wishing another incident like so many years before when my firstborn went for an impromptu swim. It was late October, and the water would not be warm enough to dip a toe in for at least another nine months, if then!

We toured the boat, while Eirik explained in Norwegian its history and then all the systems. As much as I pride myself on my Norwegian language ability, there are a lot of dialects and it is impossible to learn them all. Frankly, I found Eirik a challenge to understand.

Alisa was far better acquainted with more obscure dialects than I, so I hoped she was soaking in all the information while I spent my time examining the electronic breaker panel and poking about in the bilge.

I was particularly interested in looking at the keel bolts as rust or indications of wear could be a potentially expensive hidden cost. They looked pristine, as did the bilge itself; a very good sign.

I crawled all over the boat, looking at everything that I could think of that could cost money to fix or that might need to be replaced. And while I found a few things wrong, these were with items that were expected to wear out, such as the halyards.

In the end I concluded that the Beneteau was in very good condition, with no obvious issues. To be honest, it looked like it had hardly been used.

Alisa was bubbling over with excitement and could barely contain it. This was evidently the exact sort of boat that she had imagined owning. While Eirik was busy entertaining our daughter, Alisa whispered in my ear.

"I love it. Buy it."

"What?"

"Buy it, please. I want it."

And that was that. We went out for a test sail for an hour, and upon returning, I made Eirik an offer. It was less than he wanted and he was clearly taken aback by my direct bargaining approach.

Norwegian's tend to think things over and usually for a long time. Spontaneously making an offer on a boat the same day that you see it could be a first in this country. Eirik mumbled that he should talk to the other person interested before deciding.

In Norway, it is common to have an auction where people 'bid' against each other to buy something, even for private sales of cars or motorcycles, so it was not a big surprise that Eirik wanted to do it for his boat. But I was confident that he was not going to find another buyer as motivated as we were.

"Fine," I said. "You call him, and tell him our offer. Ask if he can do better. If he cannot, we have a deal, for my price. Yes?"

Eirik was backed into a corner. He agreed to check with the other potential buyer. He made the call, and as expected, the other party was not really all that interested after all.

Eirik wanted to get his asking price, but I stuck to my guns. We both knew that a quick sale for less money was better than a prolonged and uncertain potential sale in the future.

I pointed out that a deal now meant he would not have to pay for the boat's winter storage. He agreed, and we shook hands. The boat was ours.

Now all we had to do was work out where we were going to get the money to pay for it.

Chapter 20 – Alternative Financing

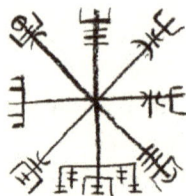

The lack of money is the root of all evil.

Samuel Clemens

In chapter five, *How to afford a boat,* I outlined in rough detail how I set about saving for Delphinus. I successfully used the exact same approach, years later, to buy Hyperion. This was the brutal, sell everything and save method.

However, now that I was far more entrenched in my middle-aged lifestyle, with two house loans, two car loans, child support and a laundry list of other things that kept me locked down in my job with no expectation of parole, I was simply not in a position to use the 'slash and burn' approach.

It seemed that I would have to be a bit more creative if we were to magically generate the necessary funds to buy the Beneteau.

So, what were my options?

Aside from the aforementioned sell-it-all style of saving, (which I have to admit, really attracts me. It is the prospect of getting rid of my possessions, which is an amazingly freeing experience) the only thing that I could imagine that might work was to get a boat loan from a bank or similar institution.

As much as I have railed against this approach in the

past, it seemed to me the only option unless I was willing to wait years while industriously scrimping and saving. Obviously, I was not willing to wait. Plus, I felt that I had to strike while the iron was still hot (the iron being my wife, of course). So, I looked into loans and what I found totally dismayed me.

In the first place, we already had a lot of debt. We had two properties that both carried 25-year mortgages, we had two almost new cars with monthly payments, a large personal loan and even a motorcycle loan, plus a good deal of additional credit card debt. I was vaguely aware of all of this, but I had buried my head in the sand in recent years and allowed things to get out of hand. Spending creep is insidious and I was well and truly within its clutches.

According to my bank manager, borrowing more money was out of the question unless I eliminated some of the existing loans first, and even then I would need a substantial down payment.

With some sadness (mitigated by the knowledge that we would be sailing in the spring) I put my bike up for sale. One less loan might make the difference, I thought. And if not, at least we were heading in the right direction. Besides, the bike was going to a better place (not a farm in the countryside where it could race around with other motorcycles) but a bike builder who planned to turn it into the most kickass of all custom café racers.

As expected, a pristine 1974 GL1000 sold quickly, and that loan was gone, along with my bike. I did not grieve as much as I had expected, since I was fixated on big boat business, and nothing makes me happier.

However, even with this small loan repaid in full, our credit was far from good enough to support a major loan from the bank.

With interest rates at around 6%, a loan of around

forty thousand dollars would require repaying (over ten years) something close to an additional thirteen thousand dollars in interest, not including any fees. This did not appeal to me, nor did having monthly costs that exceeded our combined car payments.

Furthermore, 6% is actually on the low side of the equation. I did a random search, while writing this section, and I found loan offers with interest rates that went much higher. I am not, as I have previously stated, a high finance wizard, but even I could see that this was a crazy way to pay for a boat. If only Alisa would let me sell the house!

But that got me thinking. Maybe I did not need to sell the whole house? There is something called a home equity loan. With this type of loan, you borrow money against a property you own, assuming you have sufficient equity in it.

Several years previously, I had tried to persuade Alisa that living aboard a boat was awesome, and we had bought a tiny little apartment which I reasoned would approximate life on a small boat. The idea was sound, and it really did prepare us for living aboard. When we finally got a chance to stay on Hyperion, it felt huge in comparison to our tiny home.

And although Hyperion was far behind us, we still had the tiny apartment, which we were renting out. Over the years, its value had increased considerably, to the point where we now had 50% equity in it.

There was the money we needed. We could either sell the apartment outright, or take out a home loan and use the equity as collateral. We chose the latter.

There would be no need for a high interest loan and no monthly payments. How could that be possible? Our tenant would continue to pay rent for the apartment, which covered its costs, and we could buy the boat without having to save or sell anything.

It was a brilliant solution. We got a boat that we were both happy with, even if it was not quite my dream boat (which involves bow sprits and ratlines) and it would not require us to save a penny!

If you are lucky enough to have a decent amount of equity in a property then this might be the best way to finance a boat purchase. But it is not the only way. Go back and look at chapter five again for different approaches that have worked for some people.

We signed the deal with Eirik and transferred the money to him in early November. It had been a whirlwind process. From our first discussion about boats while on vacation in Kos, to actually buying the Beneteau it had been no more than six weeks. Just in time for the boat to come out of the water before the onset of the winter snow.

It would be at least another six or seven months before the boat would see water again. Winters are long in Norway. But now I really had something to look forward to and I started making plans of where to go and what to see once the sailing season had begun.

And while this was not quite the full-on commitment to sailing that I wanted, nevertheless, I was satisfied.

If you are not in a position to achieve your dream, for whatever reason, then perhaps it is enough to get close. After all, part time sailing beats the hell out of not sailing at all.

"But," I hear you say, "What if you do not have a house that you can leverage? What else can you do?"

Well, if the slash and burn approach will not work for you, don't worry. I have a couple more ideas when it comes to finding your way to the water.

Let's say 'hi' again to Steve. Originally from Washington State, he chose to move across the continent to Maryland. Let me tell you a little about his background.

When I knew him, Steve was in his early 40s, and divorced. He did not have any children, and he had gone through a difficult and rather ugly break up. After his divorce, he ended up with a small amount of money with which to restart his life as a bachelor.

But, according to Steve, he had started with a lot more. A nice car, a nice house full of nice things and a good salary. But he also had a lot of debt. Sadly, he was not aware of this, as his wife kept her spending habits under wraps. It was *her* debt. That was unfortunate for Steve, because, according to Washington State community property laws, her debts were his, and vice versa.

After his divorce, all assets were split equally, including the debts. After Steve paid off 'his' share of the negative equity, he was left with very little to reboot his life. He decided to get as far away as he could from that bad experience, choosing Annapolis to reinvent himself. Using the lion's share of his money, he bought a cheap boat and moved aboard because he could not afford to rent anything. For him, it was more Hobson's choice than a desire to sail.

Now, it was not the boat, but rather his car that was instrumental in our getting to know each other. He had an old junker which frequently needed fixing. I could not walk past without offering to lend a hand, so naturally, we got talking.

But back to Steve. He found a job in an office, where he worked from 9-5, and on the weekends, when he was not fixing his car, he went out on the water.

Like me, he enjoyed tinkering, and was always doing something with his boat to fix it up. Once he got to the point where the sails and running rigging were replaced, his getting hooked on sailing was inevitable.

After a while, Steve did not really miss the nice car or the nice house. I like to think this is because there is something rejuvenating about life afloat but it may well have been his personality. He was a natural optimist and was quite philosophical about his experiences. He was not going to let it stop him from living his life and enjoying new experiences. Far from being broken by the divorce, he believed that it had given him an opportunity. In fact, he started to plan for the time when he would have enough savings to cast off and sail away.

In the end, things worked out pretty well for Steve. He had an adequate income, he was debt free, and he was having fun. That cheap, old boat that I had dismissed was starting to look better and better.

But for some people, even buying an old boat is not an option. Financial constraints may limit much of what we do, but they do not have to.

Consider the story of Evgeny Gvozdev, a Russian man who built a boat on the second-floor balcony of his apartment. When completed, he lowered it down to terra firma, transported it to the coast, and loaded it with food and water. Then he circumnavigated the world in it. The boat was less than 12 feet in length (3.6 Meters) and cost Evgeny a whopping 10,000 roubles to build, which at the time was less than $100 USD.

According to the Joshua Slocum Society, Evgeny entered the Caspian Sea in May of 1999. Then he sailed to the Black Sea, then the Mediterranean Sea and the Atlantic Ocean, crossing that and arriving in Chile, before finally arriving in Tahiti in November of 2001. He eventually made it back to the Ukraine in July of 2003.

This was a man that had almost nothing, and yet he managed to accomplish a world circumnavigation. His drive and determination made up for his financial constraints.

There are many creative approaches to the problem of acquiring a boat. But this idea is possibly more doable than that taken by Evgeny. If you have next no money and cannot build a boat, then all is not lost. I know of one couple that walked the docks talking with everyone until they found someone that was willing to let them liveaboard his boat, so long as they paid the marina fees.

Obviously, this requires a good deal of trust on both sides, but it could be a good idea for some.

The young couple got a home on the water, and were able to really come to terms with what living aboard means, while the boat's owner saved on all those pesky monthly dock fees.

Plus, the young couple kept the boat spotless, did basic maintenance, and promised to help with all major duties, such as hull scraping and painting. All in all, it worked out pretty well for everyone.

I think that what these stories illustrate is that there are any number of roads that will get you where you want to go.

If you find the will, you will find the way.

Chapter 21 – Self Preparation

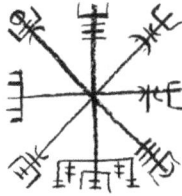

"To young men contemplating a voyage,
I would say go."

~ *Joshua Slocum*

There is no doubt in my mind that I am a less capable sailor than I need to be. The reason, aside from my limited experience with handling a sailboat in various conditions, is my weight. I am very overweight, obese actually. I remember Alisa asking me, only half joking, if I was able to squeeze past the compression post that stood before the entrance to the head. This was on the Schucker that we briefly owned in Florida. Luckily, I *could* squeeze past, but it was a tight fit.

Like many people I struggle with my weight. For over twenty years I have seen it get out of control. Naturally, I tried to manage it. In fact, I have experienced the classic yoyo phenomenon where I lose weight (as much as 98lbs on one occasion) only to regain it again, and more besides.

This is a serious issue for a lot of men and women. My weight is not just a danger to myself (heart problems, etc.) but it could even be a danger to my family, should anything happen to me while we are out with the boat.

Back when I first got Delphinus, I had to run some

rigging up to the mast. Our boat had mast steps. My concern, and an entirely legitimate worry, I believe, was if the steps could take it? And what would my weight do to the mast itself?

Okay, so perhaps it would have been smarter to let someone else go up the mast. But the way I see it, if you cannot hang upside down in a lazarette, climb a mast, and deal with any issue that arises, you have no reason to be on the boat in the first place. Clearly, I was going to have to work as much on myself, as I was on achieving my dream.

I immediately began the first of many halfhearted attempts to diet. I wanted to be ready for anything. I needed to be able to handle any situation that sailing could throw at me. After all, you need to be pretty flexible when you own a sailboat.

But being flexible is not about touching your toes (can you remember when you could still do that?) although, truth be told, that is a surprisingly important fitness requirement for a cruising sailor in my opinion. What I mean is that being flexible is about adapting to a situation, making do, and generally not being 'put out' when you don't have every little thing you want or things do not go your way. In my experience, when it comes to both boating and life, things never go exactly how you want.

This will manifest itself in many ways. From not having the right tool at hand (or even on the boat) when you are tinkering with the engine, to an ingredient you are missing for the feast you had planned to make for your guests, or even, as is currently the case as I sit here writing early in the morning, no proper tea-cup (oh, the humanity. . .)

Being mentally flexible is a critical aspect of being able to cope with the rigors of boat life. I think that if I had to put my finger on one thing, this is perhaps the most important personality trait that a would-be sailor needs to possess.

In my first foray into boating, I believe that I was flexible and well suited to a life of compromises and making do. However, Kate had been quite rigid. Things had to be 'exactly right,' for her, or they would be wrong.

During the years I lived on Delphinus I met a good many solo sailors and cruising couples, some with kids in tow. One of the most prevailing characteristics that I observed amongst them was their ability to adapt to any situation. If they had a task to accomplish, they would find a way. Not always the 'right' way either. You will get quite a few frowns from know-it-all dockside captains who will let you know that what you are doing is not 'proper,' but if it works and it keeps you on the water, then I believe the solution is fit for purpose, even if it will not get you any points with the yacht brigade.

There is another side to this coin though. Being flexible and rolling with the punches is great. But you need to be at least a bit practical with your hands.

Being a practical sailor means tackling anything that comes your way. To be prepared. I really wish that there had been a scout troupe when I was growing up. At least I would probably remember how to tie a bowline!

Being practical is a very necessary part of the sailing lifestyle, and a good deal of it is mental attitude. However, some of it is just plain old experience.

A good example to illustrate this is my old friend Steve. He took his boat out one morning, using the engine to get out of the marina. It died just as he left Back Creek and entered the bay.

Like me, Steve was a novice sailor. But, not to be

defeated, Steve raised the foresail, and made his way further into the bay. He raised the mainsail next and had a good time tacking about, before heading back, hours later.

He tacked his way into the marina using only the foresail, and made it back to his slip without incident. When he told me about it, he was so enthused that he declared that his next boat would not have an engine at all. His motor dying resulted in him gaining the confidence to dock his boat under sail. Steve adapted to the situation and gained a good deal more confidence than he started out with.

I will be honest, if the same thing happened to me, I would probably have tried to fix the engine. It would almost certainly be a fuel issue, with a blocked filter, or perhaps water in the pre-filter? Knowing how to resolve that, then bleed the engine and get it started are also critical skills, but they require a lot less gumption than docking under sail!

However, aside from taking a course in marine diesels, what else could I do to prepare myself for the coming sailing season?

Get fit. One way or another, I was going to get myself into better shape. Not by doing anything so drastic as jogging, or going to the gym. But at least by watching my diet and maybe walking a bit more.

I had about six or seven months to get myself ready for a return to sailing. Would it be enough? I had the desire, but did I have the strength? To paraphrase the good book, the spirit was willing, but was the flesh too weak?

Chapter 22 – Third Time's the Charm

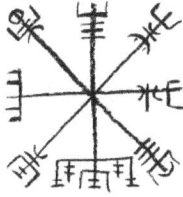

"It is not that life ashore is distasteful to me. But life
at sea is better."

~ *Sir Francis Drake*

After having waited many years, you would think that
a few more months would be nothing. Like a kid who
longs for Christmas, time seemed to crawl. But
eventually winter faded into spring and working on
the boat began to seem a possibility. I made a list of
everything that we would need to get her ready for the
water and impatiently waited for the first weekend
that promised good weather.

I made a tentative plan. Easter vacation was
coming, and that was the ideal time to prepare the
boat for launch. We would begin on Saturday morning
with the antifouling for the bottom, as well as new
zinc anodes, prop cleaning and anything else the hull
needed, then move onto general boat cleaning. I
figured that we would be done by Sunday afternoon.
That would give us Monday to do anything else
required, then launch the boat on Tuesday morning.

It was a generous enough time plan, since I did not
anticipate sanding the bottom first. We were using the
same paint that was previously applied, so it could go
straight on top of the old. In point of fact, it seemed

the bottom paint had been very effective in the previous year, as the hull was very smooth.

Part of this is due to the fact that in the colder waters of the Oslo fjord, plant growth is less of an issue. You dip a toe into the Caribbean and it comes out green after an hour. Not so in Norway! There, it is barnacles that are the problem.

But our hull was barren of those artful arthropods and surprisingly clean. And while I did not set to with a hammer to look for areas of wet core or delamination, I could see that there was no blistering on the hull. There were not even any patches of flaking paint and there was absolutely no growth of any kind. The only exception was the folding propeller which looked like it had not been polished in a very long while. It was crusty with tiny limpets, many layers thick. I estimated that it had not been cleaned in four or five years, so bad was it.

Saturday morning finally dawned, and I was ready for the drive down to the small town where we were keeping the boat. Actually, I had not really slept that night, excited as I was, so I had been ready for about six hours by the time the sun came up.

After breakfast, we set off with the car packed to the roof with everything we would need, and our first day of the sailing season officially began.

The plan went without a hitch. Almost. We used an Interlux product on the hull bottom; a thin film antifouling paint, typically used by racing sailboats and powerboats. It has a Fluoro micro-additive, which reduces friction and drag, so they say. When applied, it dries very fast and creates a hard surface. The only negative as far as I could see, is that once you use this type of antifouling, you have, metaphorically speaking, painted yourself into a corner since you cannot use anything else on the hull, except another

Interlux product, apparently.

Should you ever want to go back to a standard ablative type of paint, (the kind that wears off over time) it would require a complete sanding of the bottom and the removal of all layers of the Interlux. On the plus side, once we were done with the painting, the bottom was a beautiful, rich copper color and looked glorious.

I think we may have applied it a little too thick, since we ran out of paint before we were done. This was a problem since we did not have the money available to buy another can (it is pretty pricey stuff and payday was still a week away) plus there would be no chance of getting it before Tuesday morning, as it was the Easter vacation weekend and businesses were closing early.

As much as I did not like the idea, there was a good possibility that we might have to leave a big patch of the hull unpainted.

Luckily, the finish is very distinctive and I saw a couple of other boats in the yard that had used the same paint. I moseyed around the marina to see if I could dig up any leftover scraps of paint.

I spotted a guy painting the keel on his boat with the same paint as we had used, so I introduced myself. I explained that we had just run out, and if he had any paint left over I would be most grateful if we could have it.

Sailors, like bikers, are awesome. Whatever problem you have, you are sure to find someone to help, provide advice, or at least give a little encouragement. The owner of the boat was named Torleif, and, true to sailing fraternity form, he was willing to help.

Torleif was prepared to let me have whatever was left in the tin when he was finished. But he was slapping it on much thicker than we had and it was fast disappearing and I wondered if there would be any left at all when he was done. But finally, he applied the last stroke and there was indeed a good bit still sloshing around in the can.

We gauged the contents. It looked like there would be more than enough to finish our hull. Then Torleif stopped and thought.

"Ah . . . No, sorry. I can't let you have this. I'm going to need it for when the crane lifts the boat."

When a boat is lifted by a crane, the jack pads which hold the boat upright leave behind big square areas of unpainted hull. Of course, he would need some paint to touch up those areas. It looked like I was out of luck after all.

I nodded, and prepared to make my exit.

"Ah, yes, of course. Not to worry. Thanks anyway." I was not super disappointed. After all, it was something of a long shot. I figured that we could survive one season with our patchwork boat bottom.

But Torleif was not done.

"Tell you what. I can't give you this," he said, indicating the open can, "since I'll need it myself, but I have a spare can and you can have it."

And with that he put the brush down and went to his car which was parked nearby. He rummaged around in the back and produced another can of paint.

"Wow! Thanks! I'll repay you, of course," I said as he passed it to me.

"No need, really," he replied with a smile, hands raised as if to ward off any attempt to give him money.

I was not tempted in the least to let him treat me as a charity case, in spite of the fact that I had just been begging the last dregs from his almost empty can. I too held up a hand, in polite refusal of *his* refusal.

"No, I can't let you just give it to me. How about you send me a message on my phone, and I'll get back in touch with you next week. I can transfer the money to your account, or something."

He nodded, and produced a phone. "Sure, okay. A couple of hundred kroner should do it."

I shook my head in wonder at his generosity. A couple of hundred kroner would not do it. That was less than half what the paint cost, and this was a new, unopened can. Lady luck can be fickle, but this guy seemed to be heaven sent. I would not let him be out of pocket.

I told him my mobile number, and he sent me a message. Now it would be no problem to follow up with him. I thanked him again, and we chatted a while, then I politely made an excuse to get back to Alisa, shook his hand, and told him that I would be in touch soon.

When I returned to our boat I raised the can of paint above my head like a triumphant hunter returning with his kill. I refrained from beating my chest and making a Tarzan call.

Alisa was impressed by my sheer gall. She would never have dared to accost a complete stranger and ask for a favor.

But now we had exactly what we needed to finish the hull. I pried open the can and poured copper powder into the paint before mixing it thoroughly. Then we got to work finishing the bottom. And bonus! There was still plenty of paint left over to touch up any bare spots when the boat was lifted.

As day one of our new boating life drew to an end, I evaluated what we had achieved. So far, we had removed the heavy tarps used to protect the boat in the winter, dismantled the frame that held them up, reattached the stanchions and the lifelines, painted the bottom, moved a bunch of stuff aboard, debarnacled and polished the prop and made some new friends in the marina. We were off to a good start.

Later in the week, I transferred the cost for the can of bottom paint to Torleif's bank account, and I made a mental note to buy a six pack of beer and leave it on his boat as a thank you. After all, he had saved our boat's butt with his generosity.

With nothing urgent left to do on the boat, we spent Monday at home, wishing it was Tuesday. But the day of the launch finally arrived and we made the hour plus drive to the marina for the second time that week, Riley keeping us entertained with her constant requests to know if we were 'there yet?'

As soon as we *were* there, two of the marina workers approached, enquiring if we were ready to launch. After a brief stab of panic, we decided that we could go in the water right away. So long as we could do a last little bit of painting on the keel.

The yard guys brought a very large forklift type vehicle over, which plucked the boat up, seemingly without effort. It hung from thick straps, swinging gently.

It is a very nerve-wracking experience to see your new pride and joy lifted into the air. As most owners do, I am sure, I wondered if *this* would be the time the straps would break and the boat would come crashing down.

I hoped not, because Alisa was scuttling about below the hull, painting the last bare spots, getting under the keel to do that too, and then adding an extra layer to the leading edges on the bow, the keel and the rudder. Finally, it was finished, and there was nothing left but to stand nervously by, watching the boat pendulously swaying as it was driven slowly towards the concrete launch dock.

A short time later, and with no fanfare whatsoever, the boat was in the water. We boarded nervously, and I started the engine. As the wind was on the quarter, pushing us into the dock wall, we were a little apprehensive as we pushed off. But it went without a hitch, and we slowly made our way into the Oslo fjord.

Our first journey, perhaps as much as 500 yards, was accomplished without incident, and we made it to our slip and tied up. Finally, the boat was in its new home, and we were now officially a boating family. I could not stop grinning.

Riley was bouncing around, poking into everything, super excited to be on a pirate boat, while Alisa checked all the dock lines to make sure we did not inexplicably drift away. Everything seemed to be in order, and we relaxed, slumping down in the cockpit, letting the moment sink in.

It has been almost twenty years since I first felt the call of the ocean and it was good to know that my interest had not diminished. Sure, we would not be going on any extended cruises yet, and probably not for the foreseeable future, but knowing that we *could* made me happy.

April in Norway is bitterly cold and the summer was still a long way off, but I did not mind waiting. I could imagine years of weekend trips and summer cruises ahead of us. There was time for our daughter to grow up and to learn to sail and enjoy life on the water. And one day, there would come a time when we could plan the journey of a lifetime.

But that would have to wait. Our first job, as proud owners of our new boat, was to give her a name. Amazingly, her transom had never held a nameplate or any other marking. It was as pristine now as it was when she had left the boatyard in France.

We talked it over. Just as I had thought it

disrespectful to have a Delphinus II, I did not want a Hyperion II either. We needed something new, something that represented the family and was unique to this new vessel. In the end, we settled on a combination of our initials, one from each of us. Thanks to Riley, Alisa and Michael, the boat was named 'RAM.'

RAM is a good boat. A solid coastal cruiser, she is perfect for a small family for weekend jaunts. I had learned my lesson from Delphinus. While RAM may not be suited to heavy weather, she is the perfect boat for us, right now.

Committing to buying RAM in Norway was a compromise, but it was one I was glad to make. For me, knowing that I had the support and interest of my partner was vital. I had long ago discovered the importance of having someone to share my life with, and all its ups and downs, and I would not trade that for anything.

Almost two decades have passed since Delphinus introduced me to a world of possibilities, and finally they were once again within my grasp.

After having twice failed to live the life that I wanted, I was ready to try again. And you know what they say, the 'third time's the charm.' Perhaps this time I would get it right?

And as for Albert Einstein, while he was undoubtedly a very smart individual, he was wrong on at least one count; a man doesn't need a table, a chair, a bowl of fruit and a violin to be happy. All he needs is a boat, his family and a fair wind.

Now, where is that book of charts? I have some planning to do.

About the Author

MJ Kobernus is a writer, environmentalist and would be sailor. Although born in Chicago, he grew up in a small town in rural England. Consequently, he has a hybrid accent and peculiar views on scones.

MJ is both a novelist and the founder of Nordland Publishing. He wrote the Urban Fantasy series, *The Guardian* and the sci-fi novel *Blue Water*. His short stories have appeared in numerous anthologies, including NovoPulp, the Northlore series, Antares, the Oslo Writer's League and many more.

'MJ' stands for *Michael John,* but no one calls him that except his mother. He loves Metaphysical Fantasy, vintage motorcycles, vintage guitars, sailboats, The Beatles and Jeep Wranglers.

In spite of the rumors, he has no plans to emigrate to Mars in the foreseeable future.

You can find out more about him and his work at:

www.driven2write.com
www.amazon.com/author/mjkobernus
www.nordlandpublishing.com

Sell Up & Sail Away

213

Sell Up & Sail Away

NORDLAND PUBLISHING
Follow the North Road.

nordlandpublishing.com
facebook.com/nordlandpublishing
nordlandpublishing.tumblr.com

NORDLAND
www.nordlandpublishing.com

www.ingramcontent.com/pod-product-compliance
Lightning Source LLC
LaVergne TN
LVHW011153080426
835508LV00007B/387